100 PRESCRIPTIONS THAT WILL SHAPE YOUR PERSONALITY

Prof. P.A. Varghese

PUSTAK MAHAL®

Administrative office and sale centre

J-3/16 , Daryaganj, New Delhi-110002
☎ 011-23276539, 23272783, 23272784, 23260518
E-mail: info@pustakmahal.com • *Website:* www.pustakmahal.com

Branches
Bengaluru: ☎ 080-22234025, 40912845
E-mail: pustakmahalblr@gmail.com
Mumbai: ☎ 022-22010941, 22053387
E-mail: unicornbooksmumbai@gmail.com

ISBN 978-81-223-1425-0

Edition 2020

Printed at : Unique Color Carton, Delhi

Dedicated to

my parents and to all those
in the family who loved me

Contents

Preface

This book contains ideas and thoughts that might change your life for the best. No one is born with a grey cloud over his head and no one is destined to lead a life of poverty, depression, wants or pain. You can be successful, rich or still be happy in life, the latter being the ultimate purpose, regardless of your education, background or past. Take the first step now and the next will follow. But if you are waiting for the opportune time or a favourable break, it may never come.

The problem is with us and not with the world. Any bad situation can be made positive by reframing and you can always lessen your worry and make yourself a little merrier. Your happiness can emerge from achieving the goals you set, loving your dear ones, helping others who are in need and being empathetic with those who require your emotional support. Your relationship with your colleagues, bosses, subordinates and neighbours matters too. There are insights to guide you in these aspects in every page of this book.

There are very few in the present world who are really happy. This book will give you thoughts and directions so that you can choose the right paths to your mental and physical well-being. Cultivation of a grateful mind to the world and to all fellow travelers is a primary requisite. When you are worried about what you do not have, study those around you who are thousands of times more unfortunate than you. You need not feel sorry for anything. Instead, focus all your energies on what you cherish in life. Your thoughts, beliefs and attitude are mainly responsible for your happy or sad states of mind. There are nice thoughts strewn around to lead you to positive beliefs and positive attitude. There are practical tips to make you healthy physically and mentally and to make you live long happy and healthy. I wish you the very best.

Prof. P.A. Varghese
Kochi
Email : professorpavarghese@yahoo.co.uk;
Ph : 9895471704

1. Stop feeling sorry

What is the good in getting upset over small things which are not the way you want them to be? Worrying is not going to change the situation. There are ways to make you happy even in a very bad situation. You can recall your mind to something good that happened sometime back. You can listen to the lisping of your child or talk to a bosom friend. Now there is a trying time. Tomorrow it will all be so easy. Life is like that. It is a tear and a joy; it is a smile and a cry.

The dark clouds will swim away and the brilliant sun will emerge from behind.

There will be days which are less sunny when things just do not seem all that right. But they are going to change. There will be warming rays and fragrant zephyrs. There is no meaning in a smile if one has not experienced a tear.

Stop feeling bad about yourself. When something goes awry, do not start to blame yourself. There are such incidents in everyone's life. It is comforting to know that everyone worries too. If you are feeling bad about your terrible childhood, well, what can be done about it? Those who enjoyed a splendid one are lucky. But it is not their mistake that you did not get a good childhood. Further, they did not ask for theirs either. That is the way life is. But if you harp on your unpleasant past, no one will be interested in you. There are so many who have gone through much more trying situations. There are millions who are blind, deaf, voiceless, crippled, and mentally retarded and imbeciles. In comparison, you are thousands of times luckier and privileged.

Life gives no guarantees, but you have a choice. Spend your time brooding up in self-hate or roll over and get back to your feet and have a big laugh at the small irritants and simply march forward. Remember, over 90% of all worries never happen. And worrying is not going to help the 10% that might happen. Be prepared to face them. But there is no need to cross a bridge before you come to it.

Mark Ingles had lost both his legs in a mountaineering expedition. The double amputee managed to climb Mount Everest! *Helen Keller* was blind, mute and deaf. Still she kept a warming smile and inspired millions to go up in life forgetting all their afflictions. Our problems are small in comparison. Let us dump our troubles into the wastebasket and rise up with a heartening smile. There are so many out there much worse than we are.

2. Thoughts, not hard work, bring success

Thoughts, if sustained for a considerable period, sink into the subliminal mind to become a belief and an expectation. If they are mixed with emotions and feelings, they become powerful and are materialized very fast. That is how a lover conquers his love in a short while.

Hard work just happens with energized thoughts. There are those who toil hard but do not reach anywhere. There are those who work much less and accomplish much more. Their thoughts, beliefs and expectations make the difference. Success is not a function of hard work but a function of your intense thoughts and beliefs. The latter attract to you forces, people and circumstances necessary for the transmutation.

Even though thoughts have a power of their own, they become things only if they are in harmony with your inner self, are strong, energized and remain for long periods. Generally, they produce corresponding efforts to produce the reality. If you are thinking about creating wealth all the time, you will come in possession of money. If you keep thinking about succeeding in your profession, you will do so too. If you desire a long and healthy life, your mind will lead you to ways and means to live fit, young and strong. If you want to lead a licentious life, you will seek ways to court the opposite sex.

Irrespective of your background, if you keep thinking about becoming a millionaire, more than half the time you are awake each day for say, two or three years you will start seeing the goal coming to you. Have you heard of the statement that the world makes way for the one who knows where he is going? You should know where you are heading. You have to consciously choose your goals and start thinking about them all the time. Once your mind is fired by the red heat of a desire to achieve, they become magnetized to attract everything necessary for the materialization.

Your thoughts can be negative or positive. If you fill your mind with thoughts of poverty, diseases and wants, your mind will attract them. Thus, the poor become poorer and the sick-conscious people get sick more often. Thoughts can be transformed into wealth or poverty or sickness just like the electrical energy is converted into light and heat in a bulb. Our thoughts are working for us always, even when we are sleeping. Fill your mind with your goals and see them as already achieved. All that you think and stand for is the key to your success. ◎◎

3. Become rich with your present income!

Some years back, I was reading about a clothe-washer in the US who donated a million dollars for charity at the age of seventy. And her wealth was largely left intact. She was a multi-millionaire. She had started saving and investing one dollar a day from the age of 16. In one year, her saving would be 360 dollars. She continued doing so until 65 years and beyond. Her savings became two dollars and three dollars as her income increased but let us take the base figure and calculate how much her savings would amount to after say, 45 years. During those days, money doubled in almost five years or less. (Good investment does so even now. I am not speaking about speculative market but investment in solid companies or financial institutions). $360 became $720 in five years, $1440 in 10 years, $2880 in 15 years, $5760 in 20 years, $11520 in 25 years, $23040 in 30 years, $46080 in 35 years, $92160 in 40 years, $184320 in 45 years and $368640 in 50 years. Her second year too, saving amounted to something around this figure. The third years would be little less and so on. The 45 years' savings would be several millions. Giving away a million was peanuts for her!

When I was teaching in TKM engineering college in 1975, State Bank of Travancore had a scheme: invest rupees thousand and get rupees one hundred thousand after 40 years. I was just 25 and if I had deposited rupees fifty thousand over a few years in two-three years time I could get 5 millions now! If the investment was one lakh (hundred thousand) my returns would be one crore-10 millions - (hundred times).

Let us say you are an employee earning about Rs.20,000 month. If you curtail your unnecessary expenditures, you can easily save Rs.5000 a month. In one year, your savings becomes Rs.60,000. If you do not withdraw from it, this amount would become Rs.76.8 lakhs (7.68 millions) in 40 years, (assuming a doubling in 5 years, there are good corporations where you will be able to get this rate. If the interest rate is lower, calculate doubling period by dividing 72 by the interest rate). You do not stop with the first year. The second year's savings becomes say Rs.70 lakhs and add each year's accumulated figure for 25 years. Your 5 year saving would alone become more than 3 crores (30 millions). Compute for yourself your total worth for 25 years of saving.

The secret to wealth is continuous savings and good investment for long periods and availing the power of doubling. Your present income is immaterial as long as you save a certain percentage of it. Anyone (even with a meager earning) can become rich beyond his wildest imagination! Save regularly and increase your savings by finding additional sources of income if you would like to be bracketed with the super rich. Well, there is a long gestation period. Remember, there is no principal called something for nothing.

4. Create your future right here and now

So far you have had very little or no idea as to what the future has in store for you. You can easily create your own destiny all by yourself, right here and now.

Write down how you would like your life to be after say, 10 or 15 years from now. Take special care to note down every single detail. If you are going to write just one sentence, forget about it; you do not then know what exactly you want.

Write precisely a description of your work, the position you will occupy (mention your pay & rewards) and the details of your job or business. Note down also the nature of your work, diplomas/degrees you will take and the skills you will acquire.

It is good to draw up your proposed house with an architect (spend a few thousands) with an estimate for the same. Detail the roof, wall and floor finishes, toilet, kitchen, launch, study, façade, gate, compound wall. Have a clear and precise concept about your partner, children and where you would be settling. Note down where you want them to get educated with the names of schools and colleges.

Have a precise idea of the car you will be driving, its model and cost. Get a few pictures of it from the auto dealers. Note down, if unmarried, how your partner should be. Detail your family life, type and nature of food, parties, outings, picnics, and the way you propose to behave to your partner, kids, in-laws, relatives, neighbours and friends.

If you have finished putting down your life after 10 years in black and white, you have already created half of your future. The other half lies in thinking about it often. Let it become the predominant thought of your mind. Just before sleeping and immediately after waking up, read the detailed description carefully as if they are already achieved. Keep a copy of the neatly written details under your pillow, in your suitcase, under the glass of your office table and go through them 5 or 6 times a day. If you persist doing these and dream about them with intense desire and urge, you will get or create each one of them by the time envisaged.

5. The secret of youth at 80 or 90

There are many who believe everything is over by 55-60. Many state government employees retire at 55 and with retirement, they feel everything is over. They do not have to go to office any more or do anything meaningful and life looks meaningless. Deterioration starts from that very moment. They do not use their brain or memory; they do not exercise or keep fit their hands, legs, ears and eyes. Vital organs have started the inevitable journey to the grave.

"Why don't you have some consideration for an old man?" Many of them ask others nearby in a gathering. There are some others who tell a nephew or a niece, 'uncle may not be there during the next Deepavali' and they would die and vanish.

Well if you think you are old, you are. If you think you are finished, you are finished too. It is all in the way you think. You cannot go beyond your thoughts. They set your limits without your knowledge. Your subconscious mind programs your brain to actuate the things you think about. There is no escape from it. It is a universal law.

Devanand was past 80 when he directed and acted as a hero befriending a girl in her late teens. He was always busy planning his next project or immersing himself in the present one. *Achuthanandan*, the former Kerala Chief minister is now 86. He is still the opposition leader and travels the length and breadth of the state every day. He works more than 17 hours a day, exercises and is careful about his diet. He walks fast, and moves briskly. He keeps his memory and brain intact (he remembers all relevant facts accurately, precisely and gives apt retorts to his retractors and timely comments in his innumerable press conferences. He is trying now to get into the Political Bureau of the Communist Party from where he was expelled last year. He has very definite aims for which he is working relentlessly. He is always meticulous about his dressing and grooming.

There are so many examples like him. You can be in decrepitude or in a youthful state when you are 85 or more. Age is by far a state of mind determined by the goals that drive you and the amount of work you put in to achieve what you want. Retiring (resting at home doing nothing) is a sure recipe for the onslaught of diseases, rusting of brain and memory and the fall into death's trap.

Let us be fruitfully engaged all the time, exercise and keep our body fit, be interested in what is going around us and everyone you come in contact with and keep our vital faculties sharp and efficient. ʘʘ

6. Get anything through alpha meditation

Whatever you believe becomes the reality. Moreover, whatever that sinks into the subconscious mind becomes a belief. But how can you send thoughts to reach the subconscious mind? When you sleep, your subconscious mind is working and while awake, as your conscious mind is awake too, it is not easy to reach the subconscious. One has to reach Alpha Level to get access to it. When we are awake, our brain's vibrations are around 14 cycles per second. While we sleep, it reaches 7 cycles or lower. This stage of the brain is termed the Alpha Level. If one can reach this state while awake, whatever is suggested is sunk to the subconscious.

How do we reach Alpha Level when we are awake? Sit relaxed but upright on a comfortable chair in a quiet place. Close your eyes, take four or five deep, slow breaths holding each for 10 seconds or so and then exhale slowly feeling relaxed. Count down from 10 to 1, feeling every cell of your body getting relaxed as you do so. Now hold your attention on breathing and exhaling alone. You are now in the Alpha Level. Bring your goal statement (with eyes closed and mind concentrated) to your mind. As you repeat the same internally, do so with belief, feeling the same in each cell of your body. Feel that you have already achieved what you are stating and live in that state for a few minutes. You may also see your dear ones coming and congratulating you on your achievement. See a person whom you hold in highest esteem appreciating you. End the session by counting from 1 to 5. As you open your eyes, feel confident and happy.

Alternately, you can try this: record your goal statement a number of times in a deep sonorous voice and program the record player (as you are lying down to sleep) such that it will play the message say, after half an hour or so. You will start hearing the suggestion once you are asleep. As it will be repeated a number of times, for months and months, it creates a deep impression in the subconscious mind leading to belief. If someone else repeats the same to you a number of times while you are asleep over a prolonged period, will bring the desired result too.

There is no known shortcut to influence the subconscious mind other than through repeated affirmations. Plain unemotional words do not influence it. Emotionalize the thoughts with belief before sending them to the subconscious mind. One can overcome a bad habit, heal a problem in the body or a sickness by giving appropriate suggestions to the subconscious mind as mentioned above in the Alpha Level.

7. You don't have to know everything

Those who succeed in life are not those who know everything. Those who climb to the top of a corporation do not know every detail of every operation. A CEO should assess the risk and reward of a scenario and make a go/no-go decision. And for this, sometimes, too much information is a negative. A CEO should be the hallmark of everything that is good about the company and he should be an inspiration to everyone. Ability to delegate and decision making capability are other attributes of a successful CEO. These attributes are not based on knowing every detail or the depth of general knowledge.

Those who succeed in life will be specialized in a particular field and they will spend 14-16 hours of every day on their work. If one dabbles in everything, he would become a jack of all trades and good for nothing. The top-level executives of any corporation will have a gist of the whole. They will absorb the necessary abstract of every department and give direction to the company. If they muddle into the micro details they will reach nowhere and will not be able to carry out the chief attributes mentioned above.

If one is researching, he should go into the minutest detail of everything connected; an overall picture will not suffice. Similarly, a painter or a politician will have to master the craft in every detail. But the CMD or CEO of a corporation is set to give general guidelines and decide the direction of the corporation. He should know the pulse of the current market, the innovative techniques and the direction in which the society moves.

There is no use in gaining general knowledge. It is not going to help anyone in any profession. An encyclopedia can answer any general knowledge question. There is no need for anyone to store the data in the memory. There are quiz programs which give a million or more to the final winner. But the winner is worth just the cost of a related encyclopedia.

It is important that we identify our innate talent from very early days and acquire the necessary knowledge and skill so that our market value goes up. There are people who feel tense, as they cannot cope up with the information revolution. If you try to absorb or make yourself up to date with everything that goes on in the world there will soon be an information overload in your brain. Concentrate on your line or subject and learn what will be useful to you in your profession. Becoming an encyclopedia is worth nothing.

8. The best way to communicate

The meaning of communication is in the result. If your communication has not produced the desired result, you have not conveyed the information or communicated properly at all although, you might think you have. If the feedback is the intended result, the communication has been one hundred percent successful.

If a politician speaks eloquently for hours and hours, he may not have communicated much to the audience who would be bored to the core. A simple person would be very effective although he talks slowly and almost in a whisper. Gandhi communicated likewise. No eloquence, not much gestures, no public speaking technique. He talked from his heart whatever he believed and practiced. He had clarity (avoided ambiguity), simplicity (neither difficult nor clothed in frills and fronds), precise and to the point.

Any communication would be highly effective if one follows these simple rules:

1. The communicator must have absolute faith in what he communicates and he must be practicing the same.
2. It should be precise, short, clear and to the point.
3. It is important too that the recipient is in a conducive context to receive the information (avoid barriers to communication).
4. In an oral communication, the communicator should use appropriate body language, facial expression, gestures, eye contact and ensure that the recipient got what he wanted to convey.
5. Again he should employ modulation (use different pitches, intonation, voice patterns, stress and non-stress).
6. A lot of communication is done in a non-verbal way through facial expressions and gestures.

Preparation: Before any communication may it be a written communication, meeting your boss, subordinates or a customer, plan your talk and go through all the points to be covered beforehand. Edit the same to make it more attractive and impressive.

In an effective communication, the receiver understands the exact information that the sender intended and acts accordingly. Many problems will occur in organizations if people fail to communicate properly leading to confusion and failure of targets. ☺☺

9. Your mind, your healer

If you think about the various kinds of illnesses and fear their onslaught, your brain, nervous system and every cell in your body get a corresponding awareness that may produce what you fear, in some form or other in the immediate future. Every cell in your body is aware how you think and feel about yourself. There is no biochemistry outside your awareness. The cells of your body understand and change as per your sustained thoughts.

Fear of failure and anxiety about diseases, guilt feelings, despair and negative attitudes will bring diseases of various hues. Peace of mind, happiness and contentment will lead to perfect health. As stated, body's chemical and biological processes are influenced by your awareness. Healthy thoughts and beliefs can keep your cells healthy and young. Fearful, anxious and guilty ones will make them sick.

When you run after cherished goals with an intense and persistent desire for long life and perfect health, diseases keep away. Even contagious viruses and bacteria cannot break the immunity your system builds up. New knowledge, new skills, new ways, new aims keep your mind and body renewed and healthy.

Your mind (brain) is the greatest healer and doctor. The type of thoughts you engage in, keep away from you or bring to you diseases of all kinds. Keep always an intense desire to be perfectly healthy and to live long and youthful. No drug or medicine can match the power of your mind and its attitudes. The body follows its orders and things happen as per your thoughts, dreams and desires.

In practice, how do you translate what is described here? Have an intense desire to live long and healthy. Tell yourself every day, preferably when you meditate –'I am perfectly alright both in body and mind. My life begins today and my entire future lies ahead. I love this life and everyone I come across.' When you speak these words to yourself in your Alpha (relaxed) state, feel you are perfectly alright and let this feeling permeate every cell and organ. Feel you are like a kid who is just preparing to explore this.

10. Become a CEO

If your mind believes something, it will find out ways to make it happen. When one believes something can be done, however difficult it is, mind will figure out ways to do it. If one thinks something cannot be done, his mind will bring out all reasons why it cannot be done. If you think you can and if you think you cannot, you are right either way.

This is applicable in everything. You will find ways to overcome your problems if you believe you will overcome them. You can buy a newer and better house if you believe you will. Belief releases powers hitherto unavailable to you and disbelief brings in impediments.

If you are just pulling on trying hard to make both ends meet, you can believe you will find out a better, more paying job. If a degree/diploma/skill is required, you will take/acquire it privately continuing to work, and land up in a far better position.

There is nothing impossible. Thinking makes it so. If you believe the impossible can be done, you will. If you are a traditional person believing nothing can be changed, you will always like the status quo. You will live and die with your ordinary job if you do not believe you will improve your position or go for something higher and better. You need to dream and if your dreams are consistently focused on a single goal your mind will believe it and achieve it.

Think that you are now working in the sales department and you want to become the CEO. A CEO has to be well versed with every aspect of the company. Hence, you start taking interest in production, accounting, finance, human resource and study the functions of each in detail. May be all your free time will have to be spent for it sacrificing pleasures of idling with friends or watching TV. Think how each work can be done in a better way. Know your products, the market and reflect on the direction your company should take. This will give you more breadth and prepare you for larger responsibilities. Think constantly about how you can improve your work, how you can give more than expected of you.

11. Sex energy and success

Behind every successful man, there is a woman. Well, can we say that behind every success there is someone from the opposite sex? It is not all that common to hear behind every successful woman there is a man. Still, more likely than not, there is a man or two behind the woman.

The men of great achievement are men with highly developed sex natures; men who have learned the art of sex transmutation. Love can make you do anything for your loved one. Love is intense and passionate. When stricken with it, you excel in whatever you attempt and go much beyond your normal powers. You overcome seemingly impossible obstacles. Everything seems brighter, happier and more wonderful when you are in love.

According to Napoleon Hill, sex desire is the most powerful of all emotions and sex energy has the power to transmute mediocrity into genius.

Sex-energy is the most potential energy. When one is driven by I, he/she acquires special powers hitherto unknown to him or her. Sex transmutation is simple and is easily explained. It means the switching of the mind from thoughts of physical expression, to thoughts of some other nature. Great people resort to this mysterious force to climb up the rungs of the ladders.

If you do not love someone deeply, it can be your mother, sister, father, husband, wife, or fiancée, then in all probability you would lack that magnetic force which would be otherwise available to you.

It is known to all that a speaker would perform better if there is someone he/she loves in the audience. An athlete's performance will be enhanced by the desire to show his worth to the person from the opposite sex present among the spectators.

When the motion of love does not drive one, the driving force diminishes. In the absence of the desire to please someone from the opposite sex no one usually achieves great success.

A castrated bull loses all its charm and magnetism. It is very difficult for an impotent person to go up in life.

Every successful person transmutes sex energy into the achievement energy. It is good to have someone for whom you feel like conquering the world. That person need not be extremely beautiful or endowed with noble attributes. He or she should be able to drive you forward. He/she can be an unassuming wife or husband but you feel like making her or him a princess or prince.

On the other hand, there are so many incidents where a woman spoils the life of a man and vice versa. The choice of your partner must be judiciously done. He or she should be able to inspire you.

12. Be happy

The adventurous dive into the depths of oceans. The daredevil do skydiving or part jutting. Others tread the snow-capped mountains to reach the dangerous peaks.

Men like *Obama* spend long periods establishing themselves and again spend years giving up everything-free time, family life and life's innocent pleasures, go to every nook and corner of a large country for years, to become the leader of the nation.

Bill Gates and *Warren Buffet* make billions after years of intelligent toil and give almost the entire money they have made to the needy. Again, they amass wealth to give to charity. Millions and millions around the world work hard and hard. Peasants toil in the fields in the hot sun. There are executives who rake their brain to give direction and guidance to their company and motivate the subordinates.

What are these people after? To become a leader or the Chief Executive Officer? To conquer a mountain? To explore the sea beds? For the thrill of the adventure? To help their fellow beings? To rear up a family? Or, Just to eke out a living? Why should they become a CEO? Why should anyone crave for adventure? Why should anyone help others, especially the less fortunate? Why should people work for money?

Certainly, there is something beyond the obvious answers. If you go deeper, everything can be reduced to 9 letters: HAPPINESS. Every one of us wants to be happy. We are all equal in this. There is no other ultimate aim behind whatever man does. Even a murder is committed for the murderer to be happy (whether one will be truly happy or not is another thing). We live to be happy and peaceful.

Before we embark on anything, let us ask ourselves - will it make me happy? Let us not do something that may make another one unhappy. Sin is nothing but hurting another one and the greatest good lies in making a fellow traveler happy.

13. The impossible is possible

If you think you can and if you think you cannot, you are right either way. If you think you are deep down in a grave or if you think you are in the midst of abundance, you are again right either way.

A very difficult task is assigned to you; you may not have the knowledge. But if you say, "Yes, I will do it", you will certainly acquire the knowledge, get the necessary assistance and get it done by yourself. But if you think, "Oh, this is too much for me", you will never attempt to learn and it will remain always beyond your realm of possibility.

Sudha Chandra was a famous South Indian dancer and movie star. She had a serious accident while still in her youth, and one of her legs had to be amputated.

"I will dance like before," she declared.

"Impossible," said the doctor.

"Impossibility is not a word in my dictionary," she retorted.

The very next day she ordered an artificial leg from one of the best doctors she knew.

"Never try to balance on it without a support," the doctors advised her.

But Sudha put it on the very next day and tried to stand up without outside help. She fell; she tried again. Fell down again. Thousands of attempts followed. At last, she could stand on her own! With an indomitable will, she tried to walk but failed. Without giving up hope, she tried again and again. And at last she could walk! Simple dance steps followed. The complicated ones came after months and years of practice. At last, she succeeded and danced in a movie like the one she used to before. She proved the impossible is possible.

Anything is possible if you think so. Your attitude determines your possibility or impossibility. You might carry out anything, it may look impossible for everyone else.

14. Ring out stress and tension: ring in tranquility and peace

In the modern world, we are all always on the run: after wealth, position, possessions and in the tension we forget to live. Stress builds up and as we tend to be alone it worsens the situation. Overloading of work, politics at the workplace, lack of promotions and recognition, the melee and snarls on the roads all together our lives are on tender hooks.

Each cell, each nerve is tight and taut. The constant competition to surge ahead of others, friction between colleagues and bosses and problems in the family make our lives tense and strained. Is there no way out? Why should one go after more and more money or possessions? Wealth or possessions need not make us happy, the real purpose of life. Instead, can we not try to reduce our expenditure? Can we not try to do something we enjoy doing and do what we do in a better and more satisfying way? Can we not find time to relax, go for a brisk walk, a swim or go for cycling? Why not we sit quiet somewhere breathing slowly and deeply thinking nothing?

We come from this Universe, the basic structure of our body and that of everything else is all the same subatomic particles. We are one with this Universe and we share the universal intelligence and we do not die; we simply merge into it. We will be living forever with the Universe.

No worry, no tension and no sorrow are permanent. Day gives way to night and there is light surrounding a shadow; there is a birth for every death. The darkened sky and looming hurricane will give way for, zephyrs and light. After a tsunami, the ocean becomes tranquil and blue like a placid lake.Time heals everything. The forces that led you into the nether gloom of despair will take you to realms of pure joy.

15. Your actual age

There are three different types of ages for man: chronological, mental and biological. The Chronological age depends purely on the passage of time. It indicates the number of years passed since your birth. Mental age is the age you really feel you are. It is not related to the chronological age. One can feel young at the age of eighty or ninety; another one can feel old when he is just past fifty. Biological age is a measure of a person's real age indicating how well one is performing for their years. It depends on the functions of the vital organs, diseases one has and one's physical and mental fitness. This can be determined accurately only in a hospital. The functions of the heart, liver, lungs, kidneys, brain, endocrine glands, and those of our senses (eyes, ears, nose and taste buds and skin) have to be medically ascertained.

Mental age depends on how one feels about himself: one's weight, fat body and muscle body ratios, aerobic, static and muscular fitness, how one spends his time and the goals one follows always, can all influence it. How one keeps one's memory and brain exercised and focused is important too. If your memory has rusted, and if the thinking is blurred you have already aged irrespective of whether you are young or old and you will feel you are old.

One can reduce his mental and physiological ages but the chronological one is very independent. There are ways to reduce your age: eat less that too fruits, whole grains and vegetables, avoid processed food, sugar and salt and too much alcohol. Drink a lot of water, do aerobic, muscle building and flexibility exercises, keep ideal weight and muscle, fat body ratios. Go after something all the time, keep friendship with those of the opposite sex of any age, have a healthy sex-life, and be purposefully engaged. Help fellow men and empathize with others, live with your family or a loved one. Look for old age with warmth and plan the things that you would then do. Sleep well, eight hours in a cycle of twenty four hours is the ideal, go for picnics, give challenges to your grey matter, learn something new, exercise your brain and memory through crossword puzzles, memory diary and brain puzzles. Try new food, new dress, use your less proficient hand for your daily chores. If one keeps these points, his actual age will certainly be less than the chronological one.

16. Poverty is our making

If a child happens to be born in Somalia, it will probably die before the age of 7 out of starvation, diseases or both. A recent famine has claimed the lives of more than 29,000 children under the age of 5. 180 per 1,000 children die at birth itself. Its chances to get educated and prosper in life are bleak as Somalia is one of the poorest nations with a per capita income of $600/-.

In USA, a baby's arrival is planned much before; its parents ensure that it is provided with every conceivable amenity (good food, proper care and medical attention) and is loved and protected. It will be sent to the best schools, complete its university education and be well-placed to lead a comfortable life. Its chances of dying young is very low (infant mortality rate is only 7 per 1,000 in USA) and it is assured of the country's economic prosperity (USA's per Capita Income is $47,000).

An Indian child is probably born unplanned, unwanted and takes birth into extreme poverty. There is no food; its mother's breasts are dry (with malnutrition). There are threats to its life all the time. Infant mortality rate alone is 48 per thousand. Death rate before the age of 10 is very high. A female fetus would be probably aborted or killed at birth. The chances that it will complete high school education are bleak.

Look at Luxemburg with a per Capita income of 55,100! Its children are born into luxury; its bright future is assured by its birth alone just like a Somalian or Indian child is doomed.

What is behind all these?

Fate?

Karma?

None of them, obviously. Look at the Japanese. They have no natural wealth. Nature unfurls its fury on the tiny islands. They work hard, overcome the adversities, educate themselves and plan for the future. Japan became rich and their children are comfortable. When the settlers reached America, there was nothing but forests and Red Indians. They cleared the jungles and started cultivation. They started industries from nothing. They became rich and their children are now born into luxury! We make our nation and children's economic status at birth.

17. Convert NO into YES

'Are you an extrovert? Do you enjoy meeting strangers? Are you badly in need of making a fast buck?' If all your answers are yes, you can become a good salesperson. There are a number of new sales techniques that can make any one a success.

48% of salespersons make one call and stop. 25% make two calls before giving up. 15% do three calls and quit. 12% make three calls get 'no's and continue calling. The last group makes 80% of all sales. No does not mean no at all. Those who stop calling after one or two "no's" constitute the majority. Those who persist after a third no (12%), do 80% of all sales! See how 'no' becomes yes.

What is the thrill in selling if you get a yes at the first instance?

I took an insurance policy after saying no to the agent five times in a period of 2 years. But he was persistent and ultimately he won and me too. His pleasing nature and persistence are awe-inspiring. He studied my objections and came prepared to counter them. He was thorough with all the different policies and he could present them to me in a simple and convincing way. Once there was a positive indication in me he 'closed the deal' fast. Convince the customer of the benefit; remember you are doing a service to him. People act on two principles: pleasure or pain. Indicate the advantages he will get by buying it and pain he will have to live with if he does not. Buying is his requirement not your concern. You believe in your product, present it effectively, and bring him to the pleasure-pain awareness.

As you move to your next customer, live through a winning experience of yours. See what you saw in full colour and closer to the mind, hear what you heard louder, nearer and feel what you felt. Do not dwell on your failures. Even if you win in one out of ten, you are a success. Remember the one win and forget the nine failures.

As you move, be in your peak state body physiology: erect, shoulders drawn, looking straight and moving briskly and confidently.

Collect as much data about the customer as you can before you meet him. Find out his actual needs. Learn to ask questions and draw him to talk about his business, his life. Become a listener. Build a rapport with him and have a positive vibration throughout. Don't be pushing your product too much. If he comes up with objections about high price do not try to argue or extol your product to the skies. Just mention there is some difference with the other products and that you are not able to explain fully the reasons. But all the same you want him to buy. Keep the application in front of him indicating the place where he has to sign and keep quiet. The chances are that he will take.

18. Yes there is inequality at birth, but each one can succeed

There is a lot of luck in life. The country, state and house one is born into, educational and economic status of parents, their ability to promote their children and much more are beyond one's conscious control. One's structure of the brain, IQ, biology, energy level, physical appearance, emotional temperament, confidence levels, emotional intelligence are all transmitted from parents or acquired from one's early home environment.

The great singers, painters, poets, actors, authors have all inherited a great talent. But there is no point in crying over the bad luck or one's inadequacies. This is how the game of life is played down here. Instead, let us try to better ourselves with whatever we have. The simple reason is that our future does not depend on our past. We are not determined by our heredity and environment. We can create the future of our choice by simply dreaming what we want continuously, and taking suitable action, perhaps, until we get them.

Those who are born luckier did not ask it. If you keep harping on your cultural and social backwardness, inadequate education, early poverty, low IQ, not-so-nice looks and bad childhood upbringing, the world is not going to be amused. The world is after the winners only. You will be ignored and despised. Hence take it as a challenge and tread your way up; it may be uphill and the task daunting but there is no other way. Keep on going on; you have enough to succeed.

If you have inherited a feeble brain or if you are an imbecile, we can only sympathize with you. A normal individual like you has no excuse for not succeeding. There are those who have come up to the very top without legs, hands, eyes, and ears. Fully paralyzed (from head to toes) *Stephen Hawkins*, has become a great scientist and he occupies Newton's Chair in Oxford University. You may dwell on your inadequacies to your own peril.

19. Give less; get more

Become richer by giving a portion of what you earn or what you posses. What goes out comes back. Selfless giving ensures manifold return. All the rich people of this planet are inclined to help others. And that could be one of the reasons why they become richer. They get back what was given out in true charity, hundredfold. Giving is a sure way to receive more.

Blessed are those who can give without remembering. No wonder our present world is getting filled with those who want to give without any string attached. They are quick to part with a part of what they have earned, as they know giving has a superior value when one does so quickly and not waiting for to be asked.

The best way you can evaluate a person is by how much he gives and by how much he feels for others in his wallet. Giving is always a thermometer of one's love towards others. When it comes to giving, some people stop at nothing. 'Give all you can,' is an excellent formula for a successful life. Living for others is the best way to live. That could be why *Henry Drummond* once said, "there is true happiness only in giving." Hear *Arthur Schweitzer's* words, "There is no higher religion than human service. To work for the common good is the greatest creed."

Warren Buffet has so far given in excess of $30.7 billion to healthcare, to alleviate extreme poverty, for education and for access to information technology. *Bill gates* through *Bill and Melinda Gates's* foundation has doled out close to 34 billion mainly to the development of education and AIDS prevention. *Azim Premji* from India has donated in excess of $2 billion for education and healthcare. Every rich man is known for a charitable frame of mind (that could be one of the reasons for their immense wealth) - what goes out comes back many fold it seems.

All of us may not have the wealth, the time to do charity in a massive scale. Let us follow the advice of

Mother Teresa, "If you can't feed a hundred people, then feed just one."

20. Make yours a better world!

"You are not here merely to make a living. You are here in order to live more happily, with greater vision, with a finer spirit of hope and achievement. You are here to enrich the world and you impoverish yourself if you forget the errand." *Woodrow Wilson*

There is no point in making money and hoarding it. You cannot take it with you when you say your final adieu. We have a very short life. At the most 120 years but on an average 80 odd years after which there is going to be a veil of eternal darkness whether you like it not. Hence, live every minute, savor every moment. Let every second become a beautiful experience. There can be worries, there can be looming problems. But at this moment you have the power to be happy or unhappy.

If you feel moody, go to your favourite beach; let the sun and the fragrant wind soothe your nerves. Plan a trip for today, for tomorrow and the day after. Plan to take your kids for a movie or to an amusement park or anywhere they would be happy. Buy new clothes for your family members, buy the best automobile, go to foreign lands and let everyone enjoy living.

You might be sitting irritated over something when your child comes with a demand or childish prank. You will tend to get angry and spoil his/her day. Once an angry word has passed your mouth, it can never be retrieved. It would have caused an irreparable harm. The child goes unhappy grumbling and you become unhappy too. Why do you want to make a moment unpleasant? Hold your reaction for a minute and suppressing the natural bend of mind to be angry, say a nice word, and offer a smile. If you are doing something, stop doing it and lend your ears and eyes, lend your body, lend your mind. The attentions you give will make all the difference in the world to your child.

When an aged parent comes to your side, do not feel irritated. Show warmth and concern. After all, they gave all their time to you when you were young. They are the same parents now, the only difference is that they are no longer earning and they are not physically fit as they used to be. Your annoyance and eagerness to get rid of them will make them unhappy and if such events get repeated they will stop coming to you for anything. They will become more morose and lonely and they will start cursing their life and think of putting an end to it. In turn, knowingly or unknowingly you will feel sad and guilty. Everyone knows a feeling of hurt or guilt is very damaging to one's body and mind. If, on the other hand, you make them happy with your time and attention you will feel fulfillment.

21. Live great!

Earlier we simply looked for a job to meet our basic needs. Today we need much more: fulfillment, joy, growth and a sense that we live for something worthwhile. We want what we do to create an impact around us. If we concentrate on the value our work adds and the contribution we make we may feel satisfied. If we try to make a difference in the lives of others, we will feel great.

But the tragedy is we just drift, doing our daily chores, going for work, eating, sleeping having perfunctory sex. We are living dead. We do not feel the warmth of living. There is a big difference between drifting like a floating log of wood and living with a purpose. We are oblivious of our capabilities and forget what positive contribution we can make to our dear ones, our neighbours or to the society. Everyone walking on this planet has some special ability hidden within.

Many of us do not attempt to bring it forth. As *Ruskin* has put it,

"the weakest among us has a gift, however seemingly trivial, which is peculiar to him and which if worthily used will also be a gift to his race."

You have to identify this special gift. You have to know what you really love from an early age. Pursue the subject you enjoy, do that your mind likes. The tragedy starts when you do not follow these rules. Unhappiness results if you are engaged in something or live with someone you dislike. Or still, when you idle away your time doing nothing meaningful.

To feel really worthy, be in an environment you love doing what you enjoy. Be healthy and vibrant: exercise, eat your cherished foods (in small quantities), hear select songs and do not miss a chance to walk in the woods by the side of gurgling streams. Spending time alone in natural surroundings will mute your inner confusions and liberate your mind to see your special roles down these trodden ways. Converse with the universal intelligence and seek guidance. Read books of great minds and reflect on the eternal truths contained therein. Indulge in your special pleasures, whatever they are, without a prick of conscience. There is no sin in the world other than hurting a fellow traveler.

22. Are you fit?

Fitness is, in the simplest terms, your ability to perform well in life. We all have different goals and agendas and we must be efficient physically and mentally. A fit life is probably a lot more fun than a non-fit one. How do we know we are fit? Absence of diseases? Being lean? The feeling I am alright? It can be none of these. Some indicators are given below:

Your weight: If you are overweight, you are obviously not fit. A thumb rule is to calculate your height in inches. That can be your weight in kilograms. If you are 5'10", it works out to 70 inches and ideal weight is 70 kilograms. You can use a formula given hereunder:

J. D. Robinson Formula (1983): 52 kg + 1.9 kg per inch over 5 feet (man)
49 kg + 1.7 kg per inch over 5 feet (woman)

BMI: Divide your weight in kilograms by the square of your height in meters. If your weight is 80kgs, and height is, 5' 10" (5 foot 10 inches) it works out to 1.77M and hence your BMI is equal to 25.56. The World Health Organization (WHO) maintains BMI should be between 18.5 - 25 for both man and woman.

Your waistline measurement is also an important indicator: Take a measure using a tape directly placed on your skin or on very light clothing halfway between your lowest rib and the top of your hipbone, breathing normally. Height does not affect much this measure. As per the WHO, if you are more than 80cm (women) and 94cm (men) you are at an increased risk of some lifestyle related diseases and hence you are unfit.

Some other indicators are hereunder:

1. **Body-fat Percentage.** This is the percentage of your total body weight to the total fat weight in the body. 10-14% is good enough for men and 14-18% for women.
2. **Aerobic Fitness.** It is indicated by the ability to do moderately strenuous activity over a period of time without panting. It reflects how well your heart and lungs work together to supply oxygen to your body during the exertion. If you can climb a 6 storey building in a fast pace without panting, better raise your heart beat by 25% (if your beat is 70 raise it to 87-90 by running or brisk walking or cycling and if you can continue doing the exercise at this pace for 5-7 minutes without panting, you are fit in this respect.
3. **Flexibility.** You should have the ability to move any joint through its full range of motion. If you do not do flexibility exercises, your joints would be stiff and this is obviously a non-fit condition.

4. **Muscle Mass.** We require a certain percentage of muscle to stay healthy and this varies from individual to individual. With age, we lose muscle mass each year and hence it's important to do muscle building exercise to keep muscle mass. Sagging skin and flab is an indication of less muscles.
5. **Muscular Endurance.** The ability to hold a particular position for a sustained period of time or repeat a movement many times. If you can hold a two-kilogram weight above your head for five minutes or lift the same 20 consecutive times you get a pass mark.
6. **Static Balance.** This is your ability to maintain control of your body's center of gravity over your base of support. This ability helps one from toppling over. You may stand on one leg, hold the other leg 1 foot above and note the time you can do so without losing balance. Anything above 60 seconds is a good measure.

We are responsible for our happiness or sorrow.

It is an attitude. There are people who find peace and happiness in the midst of misery and wants. There are those who convert failures into opportunities for winning. Wealth and position may not bring happiness or peace of mind. The richest person in the world need not necessarily be happy like the one living in a hut.

The jobless think they will become happy when they get a job. But when they land in a job a bevy of problems begin to haunt them: non-recognition, work-place politics, work-load, attitude of boss, inadequate pay. High-salaried employees have higher expenses. They will have to do a tight-rope-walk with their finances. In the pursuit of maintaining status, they land up in a vicious cycle of debt. Some of the lowly paid ones have no tension; they plan and manage their lives happily, with what they get.

There is happiness in being poor, happiness in being content with what we have. There is tension in pushing for position and status. There is more happiness in giving and trying to love others than in anything else. Happiness springs from one's attitude and deeds. You cannot buy and demand it.

One can rise up from the depths of gloom. There is goodness in everything. Whatever that has happened and is going to happen is good. There is a good intention behind everything.

This moment and every moment are perfect: they are as they should be. Let us decide to be happy at every moment. If you are unhappy at any moment, you are not going to gain anything. It is great that you got a chance to be born here and live this life.

23. There is no grey cloud over your head

The world is not against you and no one is born with a 'grey cloud' over his head. The future is not the past. One can easily overcome the ordeals of childhood; the pain and disappointment of the past need not repeat in your future endeavours.

Do not let a self-fulfilling prophecy to work in your life. (If you expect bad results there is a higher likelihood that they happen.) Do not worry about what is happening to you and what has happened to you so far, but think about what you can make happen. Learn from the past and set new goals (be careful in their choice- you should simply enjoy working for them) and pursue them. If you try sincerely, some of them will yield good results and some others not so good.

Make a list of your positive qualities and achievements and post them where you can see them very often. Go through them occasionally seeing every colourful thing you saw, every sound you heard and every feeling you experienced magnified.

Start savouring everything good life has to offer. You can easily make enough money for your basic needs: it can be (annually) $40,000 in the US, Rs.600,000 in India and so on. More money need not necessarily make you happier. Stay close to your dear ones as relationships with our friends and family has a closer impact on our happiness.

Make sure you have a job you enjoy doing. Smile more; forgive and forget. Do not torment yourself with grudge or enmity. Have people around you who share your interests. When something goes wrong, try to figure out what went wrong and fix it up; do not indulge in self-pity or curse your fate. Try to be healthy through exercise, diet and meditations.

Know that every day offers new opportunities to be better than yesterday. Enjoy what you are at this moment. Nothing else matters.

The ambitious ones work harder and longer with fewer breaks. Are you always busy and still achieve nothing? Do you miss those beautiful and joyous moments of life simply because you are always caught up with one thing or another? Many feel it is good to take a little time off to look into yourself to see what is going on in your life, to think about those hours you are 'doing', to examine your work, health, relationships, just to take some time to be with your inner self. Moments of silence could be found anytime during a day to reflect on the good things that happen in life and to feel grateful to nature and the people around.

24. Learn English, the only world language

English is the universal language on the Internet, even without an official status it is already the world language. It is spoken and understood in every major city in the world and has claimed the title of global language from French with the rise of America as the super-power. Thanks to globalization, the Allied victories in World War II, and American leadership in science and technology, English has become very successful across the world. The economic and political importance of English-speaking countries have helped catapult English to the world scene.

It is highly unlikely that the position of English will be altered in the future unless the European Union or a coalition between Japan and China becomes a super power and they want to promote a language other than English. This looks highly unlikely viewed from the present context. On the other hand, the prominence of English will be on the rise and it will be the official world language. The technology of machine translation, if it becomes widespread and cheap may allow people to use their own language in international communication, English remaining the link language.

Things have already come to a stage where English is an absolute necessity for success in the world job or business markets. Non-proficiency in English will be construed a negative factor for jobs and for business promotions.

The local languages will eclipse and give way to the global language. According to researchers, only about 10% of India's or Indonesia's dialects will survive by the end of the century. There will be an erosion of the prominence of the constitutional languages of India too. With globalization, the entire world has become a single job market and without proficiency in English one's future growth will be limited or crippled. Advancements in Science and technology are accessible to the entire world population through English only. By 2020, it is estimated that at least 2 billion people will be using or learning English and it has already established itself firmly as a lingua franca. 300 million Chinese can read and write English. The other developing nations are following the example of China. Why should India be behind?

Global dominance of English can be bad news for world literature. Very few translations except those from English to other languages will be commercially viable. Only those writing in English will have a chance to reach the world audience. World literature will become English literature. See the writing in the horizon and become proficient in the language or else be prepared to be left behind.

25. Is your memory poor?

"An accurate and retentive memory is the basis of all success," says *Harry Loraine.*

Is your memory sharp and accurate? 100% accuracy is only a dream. Do you think it is sharp enough and good enough that you can rely on it? Or do you think it is rather fading? 20-25% feels their memory is good. 35-40% feels their memory is poor. About 40% feel they have an average memory.

Stop mentioning to anyone that your memory is poor. No memory is poor. It may function relatively better in a particular field and not as good in another. But it is always good. The moment you start feeling and telling yourself that your memory is good, it starts to function better. Your positive feeling sand expressions are indirect commands to the brain, and if repeated often, they will produce positive results.

Harry Lorraine says, "There is no good or bad memory. There is only trained or untrained memory, exercised or unexercised memory." Every memory is good. They become better with use and exercise and rusted with disuse and neglect. It may be true that we can remember more easily in the area of our liking. If you are a singer, you recollect songs easily. I sometimes wonder how many songs these singers can recollect with ease. They will be able to sing a song after listening to it once, twice or thrice. Great playback singers get Ok in the first take itself. The music director does not have to keep on repeating the tune repeatedly to them. Their memory is in harmony with music and its myriad permutations and combinations.

Memory remembers what one is interested in. This explains why some students score high in languages and are bad in math. I have heard many youngsters say, "I can't remember a thing of math." A boy from India will recall the stadium, city, country, year where Sachin scored a century. He has a good memory in Cricket which he likes.

If you give less attention to what you want to memorize, the weaker will be the impression and hence difficult the recall later.

It may be true that the power of memory retention slows down with age. But as its power is very high and as we use only a fraction of it normally, this does not matter at all. Memory cells are lost if you bang your head against something or if you consume alcohol or drugs. An occasional loss of a few thousand cells of the brain may not affect you as there are over 100 billion neurons and as you do not use even 10% of it.

If you exercise your mind and body and keep a thirst for life, you can recall, retain and memorize anything up to a good old age. But if you don't exercise your memory at all it may have a premature death.

Memory suppresses what you do not like or what the subconscious mind has painful association with. We always recall the names of the people we liked and forget the names of those we disliked. Mothers do not remember the details of the pain and labour but vividly recall seeing and holding the baby with every detail. The latter made her happy and the former sad.

Impression is a major factor helping memorizing and recall. How deeply is the event or stimuli impressed upon the cells? Out of the millions of sight signals that reach our retina as we walk along a new road, a skyscraper is retained vividly. Its sheer size and height must have surprised you making you look again and again at different angles. The impression or image of the object is thus indelibly marked. Whereas ordinary sights along the way is seen in a passing way and does not get impressed at all. Similarly, thousands of sound stimuli reach your brain but a few of them only gets recorded for recall. The shrill cries of a baby reverberate in your brain whenever you remember that journey. It caught your attention due to the high pitch, longer duration and the emotions it evoked in you. Its impression was stronger than that of a passing sound.

Children remember and recall better what they studied repeatedly. Repetitions make a better impression than reading once. Recalling something learnt at frequent intervals makes it indelibly marked in memory.

Interest is again a memory booster. Emotional interest helps well. Normally learning a foreign language is difficult. But if you are told you are included in a trip to china and the people of the village you are going to visit speaks only Chinese, you will be immediately motivated to learn Chinese. Without interest, nothing can be studied for retention, recall or later application. Interest can be evoked though motivation or excitement. Motivation is apt in the case of employees and excitement in the case of children.

A worthwhile goal and an intense desire to go up will help sharpen one's memory. In the absence of goals, people are drifting and they do not employ their mind or its attention on the topic and things just come and go without leaving any mark. One who has fixed his goal and walks up there or is on the move will assimilate anything he finds useful on the way with full mind and emotional involvement and he will try to recall or apply it later on thus leaving a deeper impression in the memory cells. A memory exercise is given in the next chapter to help you revive your sagging memory.

26. How to become happy?

Are you happy now? Well that is all what really counts. The richest person on the earth let it be Bill Gates, Warren Buffet, Carlos Slim or anyone else they all want to be happy and peaceful every moment of their lives. We are here to be happy. Everything points to just these nine letters arranged in this order: Happiness.

How can you be happy? This is the greatest of all questions. There are as many answers to it as there are those who think about it. When you attain a goal you are happy, even the journey is enjoyable. When you overcome your dirty habits, you become happy. When you reduce weight, you are happy too. When you live with your dream partner, you are happy. When you have lots of money, you become happy. These are all things that will make you temporarily happy. When the cause of the happiness is taken away, you become unhappy again.

How can you be happy all the time? How can you feel an inner joy every moment? If you have wealth and a bad partner, you might not be all that happy. If you become healthy, without enjoying the food you love, you will not be really happy. Even if you became the president of a company through years of hard work, you will not be happy if you do not enjoy what you do. If you do not know what to do with the wealth you have amassed, you may not be happy again. You may be healthy, you may have an ideal partner but if you do not pursue your true calling, you cannot be happy too. We can have thousands of such permutations and combinations where you end up unhappy.

How can we be happy all the time and feel the fulfillment of having passed this way?

Take this test and see how many of you have the general qualities of the happy ones.

1. Those who are happy, have fun and they feel good all the time. They would not exchange their life with anyone else's, however attractive the latter's may be.
2. Happy people live longer. Studies on nuns have shown that 54% of the cheerful nuns lived beyond 94.
3. Happy, positive feelings change the chemical makeup of our bodies, producing chemicals that enhance immunity, cell repair, and building strength. Happy people have less stress.
4. They have developed a balanced worldview and are happy they have this life.

5. Happiness and optimism go together. Optimistic people see bad things as temporary and good things as permanent.
6. Study after study shows that happy people are more likely to be romantically involved and have multiple close friendships.
7. People who are in a positive or happy mood solve problems better and faster.
8. They basically feel free to do what they want and are not restricted by others in any way.
9. Happy people want to love others and they try to avoid conflicts.
10. They are willing to cheer and help others.
11. Happy people try to be what they really are, do what they really like to get what they want.
12. Happy people are luckier.
13. They are not crazy for more money, more possessions. They appreciate and recognize what they already have.
14. Happy are those who try to get what they want and enjoy it when they get it.
16. They have something to do, something to love and something to hope for.
17. They are not, like many others, pursuing happiness madly. They live it every moment, now and here.
18. They love their work and do more than they are paid for.
19. They keep themselves fit and healthy.
20. What they think, do and say are generally in harmony.
21. Happy people take care in their dress and grooming.
22. Happiness also improves people's ability to learn and remember things.

If you conform to 17 points or more you are generally a happy person. ∞

27. Are you a successful executive?

There is a magnetism in them that is easily recognizable. They move briskly and talk low, precisely and distinctly.

Their communications are normally effective (they produce the intended result).

There will be warmth in their handshakes. They radiate a special energy in whatever they do. They connect with people easily and make many friends of both the sexes.

They are generally ambitious in nature.

They are after achievement of goals. They are not generally interested in gossips and idle talks.

They plan their work and follow the priority of work decided previously. They do not waste their time.

They are always dressed up neatly and smartly.

They are good team leaders and are good in resolving conflicts.

They are normally welcome in any group.

They take life as a challenge. They are conquerors enjoying an adventurous spirit. They love taking risks.

They have learnt the art of transmuting sex energy into achievement energy. Someone from the opposite sex normally drives them forward.

They are generally honest and loyal to their company/superior or profession.

They try to make their dear ones happy always.

They will be following the principle, 'go the extra mile' and do more than they are paid for.

They update their knowledge related to their work and are alert to innovative techniques, ideas and products.

They are careful to keep promises and compliment others.

They are generally willing to help others and try to see good in everything.

They are generally optimists. They generally learn from their mistakes and failures and try not to repeat the same mistakes again.

They generally invest in themselves and are up-to-date in their subject.

28. Wonder at the wonders around

Since my early days, I used to wonder at the world around us. The earth, sun, moon, and stars captivated my imagination and I wanted to find out more about the heavens. Deaths of my neighbour, dog and relatives made me think about life's futility. Trees live up to 900 years, turtles and whales up to 200! Our life span was less than 30 a few centuries back; it has risen in the 19th and 20th centuries due to the material and medical advancements. Majority of children born here have died before the age of 10. Why are we here for a millisecond? A rock piece lives for billions of years! The earth and the sun are over 3 billion years old!

What is going on round us? The moon and the earth are engaged in a wobbling dance which looks to us like the former is circling the latter. The earth-moon combine goes round the sun in a slightly drunken state. The sun with its attendant wobbling planets and their circling moons together moves round the galactic nucleus at 240 km per second! Still it takes 250 million years to go round once! It has circled 12 times since its birth 4500000000 years back. Our life span, in comparison tends to zero.

The earth's diameter is 12,742kms and weight 5973600000000000000000 kgs! The sun's diameter is 1.391million kms and it can contain 1 million earths! It is at a distance of 150 million kms from us. There are over 200 billion such stars in our Milky Way Galaxy! The nearest star, Proxima Centauri is 4.28 light years (4.28x300,000x60x60x24x365kms) from us. The diameter of Milky Way Galaxy is 100,000 light years! There are hundred thousand million galaxies in the Universe! And, there could be many more island Universes!

Life evolved on our tiny planet earth with its optimum size (to keep an atmosphere), correct distance from the sun (to receive just enough energy) and with an abundance of elements to the present state over a few billion years. There could be millions of earth like-planets in this Universe where life would be at different stages of evolution. There could be beings in totally different forms and internal compositions. This is a mysterious world and we are here at a corner knowing not what is going on. There is darkness up, down and around; the tottering flicker here will be off just now.

29. Run for fun

You have heard the mantra 'exercise and be fit' many times before.

"But let me say that if there is a magic to enhance the quality of your life in general: it is exercise," says *Dr. Amy Wechsler*, the author of Mind-Beauty Connection. "Exercise fights the onset of age-related diseases, lifts your spirits and sense of well-being, increases your lung capacity so you can take in more oxygen, boosts circulation to deliver nutrients to cells and skin, lowers inflammation, and, for many, it is said to be the ultimate stress reducer. That healthy glow you get after a great workout (rosy cheeks indicative of the increased circulation that is nourishing all those facial cells and tissues) isn't just for show."

There are endless studies on exercise and its mind-beauty connection. Exercise makes your brain release certain chemicals with anti-depressant effects. Regular exercise helps to extend your life. Even the middle aged people who start exercise gain extra days here. Even starting exercise in your middle age can lower death by 23% in the next 2 decades. In a well-known Harvard alumni study it was found that 26,000 people who had spent 2000 calories per week by exercising extended their lives by 2 years. Simply put, it was found that every hour of exercise would add three hours of extra life.

All of us know that exercise is good for our body and mind, but even half of us do not want to resort to it regularly. It not only energizes but lifts our spirits too. It helps every single cell of your body by producing chemicals like endorphins that make you peaceful and jovial. It is an anti-dote for insomnia, depression, and is a self-booster. Exercise helps to manage stress better and it simply promotes psychological well-being. People who exercise look toned, healthier and younger as they burn off calories. As weight reduction is inevitable, it wards off hyper tension, protects you from heart disease, obesity, back pain and diabetes. It also helps one maintain healthy bones, muscles and joints. The more sugar you burn the more active you become. It helps to boost your sex life. With the enhanced energy level and better self-esteem sex becomes more enjoyable. On the whole, it helps your entire life. It is after conducting an extensive study on a considerable number of adults on the effect of aerobic exercise on insomnia that the scientists at the Northwestern University concluded that people could improve their quality of sleep, vitality, and mood with regular exercise.

As teens do not exercise (they need at least 60 minutes of vigorous exercise daily) as much as adults these days, they become prone to many illnesses. You must have read somewhere some time that you must do 20-30 minutes of aerobic activity like brisk walking, running, cycling, 3-5 times a week. It is essential too that you engage in some muscle-strengthening activity like stretching at least twice a week. For those who have been inactive for a while, they can start with walking or swimming at a comfortable pace for short periods and slowly begins more strenuous activities. Exercise will make you feel hungry and you may eat more food but you will not eat enough to match the calories you burn. There are 700 odd exercises and workouts to choose from. If a machine is not used it rusts and before long it will die.

Our body is a complex machine and every part of it every muscle, joint and limb needs lubrication and movement. The more we move the better. As we advance in age we move less and our body becomes stiffer and the joints taut. If inactivity continues, there comes a point of very little movement and death is at the doorsteps. Movement determines quality of life. And exercise insures us. Move more live more. Inactivity and moving less erodes our mental faculties. As the body becomes stiffer the mind begins to rust. The more used and agile your body and limbs the fitter your mind.

Remember the ancient Roman saying, "in a sound body rests a sound mind."

When our organs, limbs and joints are not exercised they start giving trouble. Slowly but steadily diseases start coming in. Hospital, doctor, and medicine cripple your life. Regular physical exercise will keep away the doctor.

Those who do not find time for exercise must eventually make time for illness. Those who prefer to be in their comfort zones of idling will end up soon in the cold world 6 feet below.

All of us know what is needed to live healthier and more fulfilling lives. The sad thing is that we do not do what we know. We are waiting for the right or opportune time. And in the process weeks slip into months and months into years. Before long the sun will start casting long shadows signaling the downing of the curtain and there will be a lurking regret that we did live life the best way we could. There is no need to find a well equipped gym to begin exercising. You could start walking on your terrace in a round, as I do every day, watching the painted cotton puffs floating in the sky, savoring the fragrance in the breeze, feasting on the western picture post card like painting of nature against the city skyline, watching the crimson ball slowly lowering below the horizon. The fresh air, the chirpings of nestling birds and the slow darkening process will be, in themselves, invigorating.

30. Take the first step; the next step follows

A journey of a thousand miles begins with a single step. But without making that first step nothing will be accomplished. Once the first step is taken the next one and the next and all the others may simply fall in line. You already have enough to begin with that first step. If you are looking for alibis of 'if only' you will never really start anything or reach anywhere. If you keep on thinking about the problems ahead, you may to tend to postpone things. Prolonged delay paralyses any initiative you might have had. There is no auspicious day, there is no special circumstance; every day is right and every moment is auspicious.

All the conditions will not be just right and perfect conditions will never arrive. What you can do now in the present set-up is all that really matters. The distant and the vague appeals to the human mind as no specific action need to be taken. It is difficult to take the first steps but remember, you unleash a lot of power in doing so.

"The lure of the distant and the difficult is deceptive; the great opportunity is here," says *John Burroughs*, the American writer.

From what I know of the lives of the great, I can tell you that everything great they have achieved had begun with something very insignificant. And many people have not achieved anything simply because they failed to take that first step.

The impossible is many a time the untried. If you are in grave doubt or worry about when or how to start the journey, just take the first step and get past the starting point. Subsequent steps would follow and you may reach a point of no return! You already have enough to take the first step and then the next. Do not worry what will happen tomorrow. Take the first step and then the next and go on.

Before we begin a new venture, the whole project looks so very overbearing that we are thwarted. When you look at the long road ahead, the destination looks far away and the task daunting. And you do not feel like starting the operation at all. Suppose you are overweight and you want to reduce 30kgs! You think about the rigorous exercises over a long period of time, the food control measures that have to be implemented and you become dispirited. It is easier to be the way you are: eat whatever you want, do not exercise and it is easy to remain in your comfort zone. But all that you need to do is to just take one step now. Begin your journey. Start with a simple exercise. Do not look too far ahead or too far back either. Enjoy your present exercise.

If you have begun, you have overcome the inertia and that is a great achievement. Once you start there is a momentum to push you for a little while and a few steps would definitely follow. You have to get charged up by motivating yourself with the goal thereafter. Once it is an intense desire more steps would follow. March on never losing sight of the finish line and never looking back. When I was a faculty of the TKM college of engineering in 1976, State Bank of Travancore had an offer: deposit Rs.1000 and get Rs.100,000 after 40 years. I thought about it for a long time. But looking so far ahead into the future everything looked hazy and impractical. I held on with the idea for quite some time but never took the first step. And the result: I saved nothing. Now after about 40 years, I regret having not taken that first step. I could have easily deposited Rs.50,000 over a period of a few years and I would have been a millionaire now!

We hear people talking about big plans over and over in life. There are so many who want to write books and become famous, others who want to start a big business, and still others who plan to build a mansion. They are all waiting for the conditions to become right, for the auspicious moment. Very few realize that every moment is auspicious and every day is the right day. The conditions are not going to be different from what it is now the next year or after ten years. If you do not put that first step, you will never achieve what you want. As in the case of my savings plan I would have been closer to my goal had I acted on time and started depositing my savings in the bank. If you wait under whatever pretext, the goal would recede further and further without any change in your conditions. Winning is the most important part of any endeavour. Non-starter is worse than a quitter. 90% of success lies in starting, in taking the first step. You may fail after starting but you have a chance to win. If you do not start, you are doomed as you have no chance to win. The first step is the hardest of all. Many of us fail because we do not take that first step. We do not overcome the inertia. One step is all that matters. If you don't grow, you whither; no one can stand still. In other words, you will never do great things if you do not do small things. The courage to begin is the same as the courage required to win. Little by little is a universal rule. Doing small things like taking that first step makes all the difference in life.

31. Invest in yourself

During a seminar for MCA students in 2001, I asked them, "Why did you opt for MCA?" "We will get one hundred thousand rupees when we pass out." It was surprising that none of them mentioned his innate interest in the subject. A few had a liking for computers. 4 years later, I was on the interview board of a medium sized electronic company and there were more than a hundred candidates for the post of junior programmers. We tried to know what they knew about programming. The vast majority had not applied what they learnt in the text books. Passing the exam was their sole interest and they were not bothered about the practical applications or appropriating the knowledge. The university degree was all that mattered and once the exam was over they forgot most of the theory too. "How much do you expect? We asked those who fared better in the interview. "Will you give Rs.3500 ($70 a month)?" I was surprised as they had dreamt of Rs.100,000. Why did they come down to less than one-twentieth of what they had dreamt of?

When posed with this dilemma Kerala Participants would answer; "they wanted a job at any cost as jobs are hard to come by." But was unemployment the real reason for bringing down one's value? Many of their own batch mates had been absorbed by Infosys, TCS or Wipro at much higher pay. It was definitely possible to get more. But higher salary would always go with higher expectations. One had to invest in oneself to have the courage to ask more. Those who by-hearted the prescribed text a few weeks before the exam and vomited the same into the answer sheets would be diffident and accept any offer. Most of the two years earmarked for the course had been squandered walking around the campus, commenting girls and boys or engaging in silly endless conversations with friends, seeing every movie released, going to the city centre in the evenings in the company of others, or daydreaming. They attended the classes perfunctorily to get adequate attendance and to pass in the personal evaluations by the teachers. Mind was not in the subject, they were not investing in themselves.

During my career as a CEO, I had to interview a number of engineers. We would go in depth to see what they really knew on the subject. After the interview, each of them would be asked for his/her salary expectation. They would ask for a little lower than what we had advertised. Why? The old theory that they wanted a job at any cost does not hold good as we had published the salary. Then? They felt they deserved less. They felt they were not worth the salary the company was willing to pay for the post. From my experience I have gathered that an interviewee would ask more and stick to it if he were confident in himself. These guys with 5-7 years of experience in the construction industry had not invested in themselves, they had not tried to learn what they did, they had not gone into the net to study the latest methods and modes of work, they had not thought about increasing efficiency or cutting down cost. They had not put their heart and soul to do the job with utmost quality and perfection and above all they did not try to grasp all the related aspects of construction and upgrade themselves so that they could handle any responsible position in the industry.

We waste a lot of our time. If we make a simple time analysis of the way we spend each minute in our lives it would be easy to find that of the 24 hours available to us each day, we will be wasting about 3-4 hours or more. This includes time in front of the TV, sitting idle or day dreaming, chit-chatting with friends, boozing, going for movie, or loitering around the city center. Even while we travel we can make use of the time by reading, recollecting, or thinking about our goals. We all invest money in the banks. But how many of us invest in ourselves? Is that not the greatest investment? Let us acquire more knowledge, more skill and more ability in our chosen field. There is no greater crime than wasting our personal time. Invest in ourselves by learning more about what we do or through the net (every knowledge is there) or through a short term course and thus let us empower ourselves and command more pay and perks. Let us equip ourselves so that we are more valuable at the market place and at home. I think we decide our price. And today or tomorrow we will be paid what we are worth.

32. Are our problems all that big?

In an earth like planet with the optimum gravity to retain an atmosphere, at an optimum distance from the sun (to get just enough energy) with an abundance of elements life has to be evolved and there is an advanced civilization flourishing down here. There may be millions of earth-like-planets in the Universe and there could be life in many of them with advanced but alien civilizations. But we will always be alone here as the distances involved are too massive that there is no way another civilization can become our friends or foes. But life has to end before the demise of our own sun which is not far away in the astronomical time scale, a few billion years from now. Our sun would start expanding and end up in a supernova and a dark curtain of death will befall the entire solar system including the earth. Life on this planet will end forever. Life, if it exists at other planets of other stars, will end too with the demise of their respective stars.

Thousands of billions of people have taken birth here and gone. A majority of them died before they reached the age of ten or less. Millions died in wars fought for gods, religions and nations. Billions have perished in natural calamities and they still do. Deadly diseases have devoured legions. No one is alive now whose age is more than 125. That is our maximum life span, but this small planet has been there, almost in the same form, for the last 42000000000 years! It may be there for another 40000000000 years!

We humans are like an air bubble, forming and bursting out almost simultaneously. We are so insignificant and infinitesimal taking in a breath and breathing it out for ever. From this perspective, are your troubles really that big? Are your past, sad experiences, the problems you currently face and the challenges in front of you really as big as you think them out to be? We walk down here on this planet for such a short while. On the overall scheme of things, our lives and their myriad problems are all just blips or less when we see them from the perspective of the Universe and the eternity of time. Hence, let us enjoy this sojourn and savour the short travel on the surface of this interesting globe. We have this life at this juncture of advanced civilization; we are able to enjoy the fruits of all scientific discoveries and material progress. So keep a smile now and give a hand to your co-travelers. There is no greater joy than having obtained this breath, this life.

33. How do you select a partner?

"Why do we feel attracted to someone at first sight?" You do not know him/her or the background, family religion, views, likes, dislikes qualifications, job status, nothing. All the same you just felt attracted instantly. Need not be a 'thunderbolt love', but some unknown strings pull you to him/her. Sometimes you feel like you have made a connection. You looked at this one person out of the entire people assembled there and thought, "wow! This person is made for me!"

In countries like India, dating or living together before marriage is unthinkable and consent for marriage is very much based on the first-sight- impression and a few words exchanged largely in the presence of the elders. (Even in societies where free-mingling is an accepted norm, the first liking always happen in an identical fashion which leads to a relationship later.)

When you meet a group, you like some of them; you dislike a few others and a third category does not evoke any particular emotion in you. Dressing, appearance, body physiology and grooming do differentiate them, but that may not be the real reason that has brought these reactions in your mind.

You instantly like one who has similar features to someone who was dear to you during your infancy and early childhood (these features are all indelibly inscribed in your subconscious mind). Further, from your life experiences you have drawn a list of the nature of the characteristics ('criteria') like the colour of the skin, height, weight, facial appearance, hair, body profile, body language and communication that strongly appeal to your mind. If you find these criteria and the features in a particular person you tend to like him. This is universal, and it has no east west or south north divide.

This is an unconscious process and it does not result from any objective study of the person in question. The first attraction will create a lasting mental bias towards him or her and unless conscious efforts are later undertaken to correct the same, you are positively inclined to the one who matches with your map and criteria of the ideal person and negatively inclined to another who is a mismatch. There is no effort made to study whether your views, outlook on life, emotions and others are compatible. The strong sexual attraction conveniently hides the differences and you become passionately involved. An impartial assessment of one's nature and personality is very difficult. The real colours will surface only after the consummation of marriage and no wonder half of all marriages end up in divorce.

34. Your profession: let it all be play and work

One of the timeless secrets of a long happy life: pursue a work that you can enjoy. The common denominator of the happiest souls is that they all loved their work. It was fun for them. They did not work a single day. It was all play and work. The truly successful ones simply pursued their goals without knowing whether they were working or playing.

This is the greatest criteria you should bear in mind. Not the pay and perks. Not the management and the working climate. Not the scope for promotions or personal aggrandizement. Not the pension or the distance from your home or anything else. It need not be a regular job; you follow what your mind is after. It can be photography, singing, painting, bird–watching, animal or plant love, nature conservation, fashion, movie direction, sculpture, selfless service, whatever. The question is: 'Will you enjoy doing it? Will you be able to develop a passion for it?' Chose a profession which you will enjoy, which will be like a hobby. This should be the only guiding principle in choosing your work or goal.

When you love what you do, money will start coming. Don't worry about it at all. If, on the other hand, you went into a profession attracted by the pay, perks and other benefits, you will regret it the whole of your life. That will be your greatest sorrow before dying.

35. Can we prevent natural calamities?

In a sense, thoughts are things and the prolonged, intense thoughts do become things. A building is first conceived as an idea before it is transferred into a paper and then into the ground. Everything that we see down here began as a thought. The whole civilization has been made real through man's imagination and his thoughts. But all that happen on this earth are not brought about by thoughts.

There are natural disasters like tempests, hurricanes, earthquakes, famines, volcanic eruptions, floods, pestilences, epidemics and plaques which occur as per the inherent physical, gravitational and chemical laws of this planet, the solar system and the Universe as a whole. No one including god can prevent or produce them. The forces involved are colossal, beyond even the reach of human imagination.

Yes, conscious, energized and persistent thoughts always become reality or whatever one visualizes for long does happen. The energy and the mental vibes will influence nature to attract forces, healthy centenariane and circumstances that will help in the transformation. The brain vibrations will interact with the universal energy and the invisible thing becomes tangible.

But it is erroneous to say that 'things are thoughts.' Natural calamities are also forms of energy.The forces are massive and huge. Nobody can bring or stop a volcanic eruption or an earthquake or a hurricane. Let us say one focuses all his thoughts on stopping an earthquake. His thoughts produce some energy, but it is negligible in comparison to the massive tectonic forces involved in shaking this earth! Even if a billion people concentrated upon the desire in absolute harmony and channelized their thoughts on the target, it would amount to almost nothing in comparison.

A thought produces infinitesimal energy. A million peoples' thoughts of a day or a month or a year will not produce any significant value to affect a natural calamity. Everything in nature follows the laws of the Universe. Bigger forces overpower smaller ones. Who can stop the earth spinning around the sun? It has been doing so for over 4200 million years! It has to continue its revolution and its rotation around its own axis so far as the overpowering sun's gravity lasts.The sun, with all its attendant planets and their moons, is revolving around the galactic nucleus with a speed of 250 kilometers per second! It cannot stop this either. Everything on this earth are produced by an infinitesimal portion of the sun's energy that reaches this earth. The 'poor' little humans down here cannot prevent natural calamities which are powered by the sun and the changes happening on the earth's core and its mantle. Man has to produce colossal amounts of energy to bring about any change and as he can never do the same and natural calamities will continue. ☺☺

36. Are the laws for the poor and the weak?

The rich and the powerful are above any law. They, with their money, power and connections will always find a way to come out clean with a 'not-guilty verdict'. The poor are hooked by the long arms of the law-enforcing agents and the judiciary. Without adequate resources they cannot find a good lawyer to present their case and in many instances, the mighty criminals go scot free and the poor get punished! Remember half of all the people in India are in abject poverty!

Why is it that a government official, minister or leader rarely punished or sent to jail in any one of the cases involving bribe or cheating? The law can be twisted in their favour; there are innumerable loop holes for the rich and the powerful. They have the wealth and the connections.

Further the poor slum dwellers and those born to criminals are more inclined to commit a law-violation than the rich and the well-bred. The former have to, sometimes, resort to stealing or prostitution just to survive. There are so many who get a criminal tendency through their genes. There are others who are forced into gambling or drug-trafficking. Righteous parents will bring up law-abiding and morally good children with strict moral codes. They discern right and wrong and develop a conscience which prohibits them from committing a wrong. Children of the criminals, underworld dons, the slum dwellers, the petty thieves and prostitutes will violate laws more often knowingly or unknowingly. Where genetic aberrations exist 'crimes' cannot be helped. From this perspective, equal application of law to all looks totally meaningless.

No law enforcement agency arrests a high society lady who gets the services of gentle-men in a 5 star hotel. But the poor who does it in a third rate lodge is caught red-handed for adultery. A higher-up who uses a costly prohibited drug cannot be caught as the one on the street who has to openly inhale the fumes of Ganja. A government minister who manages millions of rupees through illegal activities is uncaught while a petty thief who steals a watch worth Rs300 ends up behind the bars.

37. Offer challenges to your grey matter

If you keep on doing the same thing in the same manner and live a monotonous life daily, your brain would lose its sharpness and you will start ageing fast. Here are some suggestions.

Try new foods. Why not you walk into a Japanese restaurant to eat cooked rice and a slice of raw fish or a Vietnamese one to taste a piece of a snake or a reptile? Or experience the pungent spicy curry in an Indian restaurant.

Get away from the rut of eating the same food you have been eating all the time. Let there be challenges to your brain. Try wearing a Japanese Kimono, an Indian dhoti and a Nehru shirt, saree and blouse, or a unique African traditional dress. Let your brain adjust to the queer feeling and live with it.

Take another route (other than the one you go every day) to your house, go to different churches, night clubs, restaurants, supermarkets and different tourist destinations.

Choose a different seat at the dining table, eat with fingers without fork, use left hand to brush, iron, and write (the last one requires practice) and try a new set of casual ware at home.

While at home, walk closing your eyes (let your brain adjust to the no-sight situation) and try walking backward. Give more and more opportunities for your brain to become active and use its untested powers.

Maintain a memory diary and record in it the people you met today in the order of meeting. Or, record whatever you did sequentially (especially if your memory is weak). Try to recall the names of those you met last week at the supermarket or at the church or at the wedding reception. Recall the places you visited and even saw during your last trip abroad. Bring to your mind every detail on the sides of the roads you have travelled.

As *Harvey Ullman* observed, "Anyone who stops learning is becoming old".

They are staying at a fixed point of time. They do not experience anything new; they feel the advancement of age and the approaching death. They idle away their time waiting for the inevitable to happen. They do not pursue a new goal; they deteriorate by stagnation. There is only one master key that can unlock your future and lift you up from the morass of drudgery: dreams, goals and the desire to achieve them. Find dreams worth chasing and go after them. If it can captivate your heart, your focus will be sharpened and you will attain a new momentum in the hot pursuit.

38. Laugh your way to health

We know our health very much depends on our mental condition. When we are in the company of good people or are in cheerful surroundings, our body functions much better. Unpleasant scenery and the presence of those whom we dislike can make us sick and tired. A steady, good state of mind can usher in health and a negative one in sickness.

Mental states influence our nervous system and vital organs. One can acquire radiant health with a bit of exercise and food control coupled with a positive state of mind.

It is now proven mental disturbances like anxiety and tension can induce diabetes, asthma, bronchitis and even blood pressure. Acute depressions and intense grieving can induce cancers! One's feelings, emotions, and mental states reflected in one's brain waves, influence our health. Simply put, mind has a lot to do with one's physical state. By controlling one's mind one can be healthy.

Depressing and negative thoughts force our glands secrete poison into the blood. It affects or retards the normal body functions like circulation, digestion and assimilation. A pleasant state of mind induces positive secretions which facilitate all these functions.

Constant laughing, smiles and a joyous state can cure diseases and help our body build up immunity against them. If one is depressed or sad, immunity gets reduced and the count of the white blood corpuscles comes down. In a recent medical research, cancer patients were accommodated in a hall where they were allowed to read only funny magazines, articles, anecdotes and books, and see humorous films or videos. The experiment was continued for six months. When they were tested afterwards, it was observed that almost 20 percent of the patients were cured totally! There was a marked improvement in the others!

If a continuous joyous state can cure even incurable diseases like cancer, ordinary illnesses can easily be overcome even with occasional smiles and a positive state of mind. It is also proven medically that anger, frustration and sorrow can bring in diseases including cancer. Widows, for instance, are much more prone to breast cancer than others. A pleasant state of mind is conducive for health and well-being. The facial features can change one's inner state of mind. If your facial muscles can be turned into a smiling state, the intensity of sorrow will lessen and it will help maintain a pleasant state and build up disease fighting mechanism. So, keep a smile always dangling on your lips.

39. Attain super health

There is no point in living without being healthy. Does your health depend on the treatment you receive to cure your diseases? Does it depend on the number of times you visit doctors or hospitals?

Doctors, hospitals and medication can only help you get rid of symptoms of diseases. And absence of disease does not mean good health.

There are 3 stages in this regard: diseases, absence of diseases and super health. Generally people are worried about the first stage and are interested in the second one. Super health is perfect mental and physical well-being. Very few are even aware of the third stage and still less know that it is purely based on a personal initiative.

You can be mentally and physically fit only if you want to, only if you think and intensely desire it. Medical examinations and tests will reveal certain parameters like blood pressure, sugar and cholesterol levels in the blood, the onslaught of cancer, AIDS, or any other disease and the way your heart, lungs, kidney, liver or any other vital organ functions. The doctors will advise you as to how to get rid of adverse symptoms and prescribe medication to get rid of them.

But no doctor can make you healthy. No medication can ensure your mental and physical well-being nor can it induce youthfulness and energy. NO ONE ELSE CAN LEAD YOU INTO SUPER HEALTH BUT YOU.

Your thoughts will decide whether you will be healthy or sick, young or old.

May be the following checklist would help:

1. Do you have an intense desire to live long and healthy?
2. Do you have a life goal or goals which will drive you forward and make you fruitfully engaged always?
3. Are you fit mentally and physically? (Do you exercise regularly and control your diet eat generally less, eat more vegetables, fruits, whole grains and nuts; take less salt and sugar, drink more water; avoid a lot of fatty or fried foods)
4. Do you exercise your brain and memory on a regular basis?
5. Do you feel like involving yourself romantically with those of the opposite sex of any age?
6. Do you enjoy your life and feel grateful to the forces that gave birth to you?
7. Do you take care of your personal appearance, go for picnics and keep friendship with likeminded people?

If you do all these, you are on your way to super health. ☺☺

40. Beat procrastination

Lazy people only think of doing things tomorrow or the day after. Problems and tasks are simpler or easier if you tackle them right now. Putting them off often ends up in you never doing it. Some of us wait and wait until the entire things have just disappeared. If you find somebody who brags about what he is going to do tomorrow, probably, he did the same thing yesterday too. He will only brag and never do anything substantial.

There is a saying, 'Tomorrow is the only day in the year that appeals to the lazy man.'

Why do you put off things?

Because the work is unpleasant or difficult or still you do not know how to do it? If the reason does not fall in one of these, you do so as you are lethargic or simply lazy. If the task is difficult break it down into smaller elements so that each one does not look formidable. Generate adequate interest to get the work done at any cost.

If you have too much to do, prioritize the whole thing. Do the most urgent ones first and so on; if there are still tasks to be completed assign them as the first priority of the next day.

If you have the habit of postponing, it will erode your self-esteem and confidence. Whatever is to be finished today has to be finished today itself. If you procrastinate for tomorrow, you will postpone it for the day after and then for the next day. The task will remain unfinished. If procrastination becomes a habit you are in a dangerous web of never accomplishing anything.

A common complaint for postponing is lack of time. This is only an excuse, a lame one at that. Because you have solid 24 hours each day like Mother Teresa, Leonardo Da Vinci, Abraham Lincoln, Michael Angelo or Gandhi. They accomplished so much and we are postponing our daily chores!

There is another beautiful principle. Time expands or contracts with work. If you have more work at hand, you finish each one faster. If there is very little to do you tend to take more time to finish a job requiring much less time. It is all in your hand. If you want to complete the entire work it can be finished on time.

If someone says, 'I do not have much time,' it only means he does not have much interest in that work. If one has genuine interest you will find time somehow. It is always lack of enthusiasm or direction and not lack of time.

41. A legless legend

Mark Joseph Ingles, born on 27 September 1959, is best known legless mountaineer of the world, He is also an established wine-maker, cyclist and motivational speaker. He had persistent dreams since his boyhood to stand at the top of Mount Everest. He started climbing mountains in right earnest since he was a little more than a boy. But in 1982, a great tragedy struck. He got stuck in an ice cave near the peak of New Zealand's majestic Mount Cook. As a result, both his legs had to be amputated below the knees due to frostbite.

He did not give up. He doubled his efforts on artificial metal legs and in 2006, his dream came true and he stood on the roof of the world- the summit of Mount Everest. He was the first double amputee to do so. Through this indomitable courage, he not only proved that anything is possible for anybody regardless of insurmountable obstacles but he also collected thousands of dollars for the double amputees of the world.

He has a degree in human biochemistry and worked as a wine maker for more 10 years. After the accident he was active as a cyclist and was an ardent skier. He got several medals in the Sydney 2000 Paralympics. Later, the mountains beckoned him back and he scaled Aoraki Mount Cook in January 2002. In 2004, he was at the summit of Cho Oyu, the 6th highest peak in the world. From this summit he looked straight out at what people had told him impossible, Mount Everest. And he made history by conquering it without legs!

He wants to make a difference in life and is not satisfied just being a voyeur. He pursues lifelong learning. He takes challenges head on and overcomes every stumbling block that comes his way. And his wife Anne, and their three children Amanda, Jeremy and Lucy are all a constant sources of inspiration and support for him.

Of late he has been inspiring people to excel through presentations to corporations, schools and community groups. He uses the lessons he has learnt to push the limits further. He is out there to support a lot of people who are in dire need of help. He wants to help the 400 million disabled people of the world! He has established in New Zeeland a charitable trust, Limbs4all, with this in mind. He has also arranged artificial legs for the Sherpa's who lost theirs just as he did. To raise funds he conducts a number of activities including risky trekking adventures in the mountains of Nepal. *Mark Ingles* is a remarkable person of indomitable courage and is role model for all who want to achieve success in this life.

42. Cultivate a world view

We live on a minor planet of an average star located in the outer limits of the Milky Way Galaxy which contains over 200 billion stars. All the planets with their satellites revolve round the sun which in turn along with all of them goes round the galactic nucleus at a very high speed.

There are over one hundred thousand million galaxies in the Universe! Scientists think there are a number of such Universes! Against these scales, even our Milky Way Galaxy, (dia.100,000 light years) wherein our own sun is just an ordinary star is just a speck or a dot; our sun a negligible object and the earth infinitesimal.

In an earth like planet with the optimum gravity to retain an atmosphere, at an optimum distance from the sun(to get just enough energy) with an abundance of elements, life evolved through random chemical reactions and later, through evolution, reached the levels of an advanced civilization we see today. There can be millions of earth-like- planets in the Universe with life in many of them. Due to the huge distances involved, we do not know each other. The entire solar system and the life on planet earth will end with the death of our sun in a supernova after 4 billion years.

Thousands of billions of people have taken birth here and gone. A majority of them died before they reached the age of ten or less. Billions have perished in natural calamities and an equal number in wars fought for gods, religions, powerful guys and nations. No one over 125 years is alive today. That is our maximum life-span. But this small planet has been there, almost in the same form, for the last 42000000000 years! It may be there for another 40000000000 years! But we humans are like an air bubble, forming and bursting out almost simultaneously.

Man evolved from the lower mammals like chimpanzees probably in Africa and later spread out to the different continents. Geography and climate made him black, white, yellow coloured with myriad physical linguistic and cultural differences. Temperate areas advanced more than the hot climate ones; Regions like America, northern Europe, Japan, Korea Australia and New Zealand are all rich and prosperous. Sub-Saharan Africa and Sothern Asia are poor and underdeveloped. Ethnic, nationalistic linguistic and religious differences have brought about innumerable conflicts.

Man's life had been extremely difficult in the early years. Food was scarce and he had to face the fury of nature, diseases and death. But his powerful procreative faculties made him survive and proliferate. He tamed animals, discovered agriculture, developed industry and started to make his life comfortable in the recent past.

During the early stages of human evolution he was awe struck at the wonderful nature phenomena. Many of them like the sun and moon were good and he started making them benevolent gods (deification of nature phenomena).The forces which caused floods, hurricanes, thunder & lightening, earthquakes, volcanic eruptions, contagious diseases and plagues became evil gods. He started pleasing the former and appeasing the latter.

Further he was puzzled at the death of a friend who was walking with him just the other day. Something must have left his corpse (the body remains intact after death-at least for a small period) and naturally he started thinking of a spirit that must have left the corpse. This is the beginning of animism– the cult of the spirits. Man was sad of his mortality and he longed to live eternally like the gods he made. All these together laid the foundations for the various religions we see today. Millions of gods of all shapes and hues got evolved and some of them became superior to the others. Later, in tandem with the rise of powerful kings and emperors, the concept of a supreme god evolved too. Religious leaders of different natures established different ways to live here to please his gods. Buddha, Sankara, Christ, Mohammed all had their own versions.

The discovery of agriculture and evolution of human societies made religions organized too. Today we have atheistic Buddhism, pantheistic Hinduism, monotheistic Christianity, Judaism and Islam, atheistic communism, and animistic beliefs. There are hundreds of warring sects for each one of the major religions. Religions have caused thousands of wars, communal strife and they have harmed the peaceful co-existence of man.

Parents program children to believe their religion. The brain washing is so intense and deep rooted that normally they come to believe their religion is the only true one. Perhaps it is interesting to note that these religions are fundamentally different in the concept of the god, how man should live here and the nature of an afterlife. Even the ultimate purpose of life varies totally from one to the other. For the Hindus, it is cessation from the chain of birth and rebirth, for the Buddhists it is Nirvana or total detachment, for the Moslems it is a material heaven where every conceivable pleasure is available and the Christians speak of a spiritual life with the godhead. Even today, in the midst of an advanced civilization half of all men still believe in a religion of some sort, more due to the force of habit and early childhood programming than due to any other cause.

We have these enigmatic 100 odd years in front of us. We can live it in the delusion of a god, heaven and do everything for the afterlife. Or, we can understand the true facts of life and face things squarely living this life happily and successfully with a lot of celebration, helping fellow beings and at last go with a gratitude that we got a chance to come down here.

43. You need not age after all

There may be a clockwork mechanism that makes us aged. But with a proper life-style, one can extend one's youthfulness well beyond 100. All our limbs and organs can function well up to 120 years! It is our mental outlook which invites ageing.

Decaying is a universal phenomenon. But our mind can control the decay of our body tissues. It is not fully true that old age leads us to death. Death is brought about by diseases like BP, cancer, heart attack, TB, Pneumonia, AIDS, accidents, illnesses, and in rare cases by old age. The thought that one will have to be senile and useless in old age is totally unfounded. There are people who enjoy youthfulness in old age with all their organs and limbs functioning well up to 110 and more.

It is not necessary that because one is decrepit at 90 another should also be decrepit. If you exercise your body and brain, control food, and live for certain aims, you can be as healthy at 95 as another one is at 60.

Eating less (take food equivalent to 1200 calories a day) can add up to 50% more to your life span! Studies have conclusively shown that taking a serving or two of broccoli each day, one can add 5 years to his life. Having a pet and spending time with it regularly can give you 3 more years. If you live in a rural setting amidst greeneries and with a lot of unpolluted fresh air you will get 7 years more! Having an understanding and loving partner will extend your life by about 5-7 years!

Leaving your memory and brain in a rut (doing routine things which give no challenge) make them rusted and they prepare to die earlier. Brain is a self-programming mechanism and if there is no use staying alive it just goes.

If you exercise physically and throw new challenges to brain (doing puzzles, going to new places, studying a new language, doing your daily chores with the less proficient hand, writing memoirs, recalling names of people you met, doing memory games and living for a purpose) it will function like a youth's brain.

This is applicable to all our muscles and organs. Keep them exercised and let them be fit. Go for aerobic, muscle building and flexibility exercises. Nobody can stop chronological ageing but your mind will behave like that of an youngster if you exercise your body and brain, move more, control your food and have something to live for.

44. Reach the top at 35!

I have read about very young guys who joined a corporation as trainee manager when they were 21 or 22, just after graduation, and became the CEOs at 35. There are 500 or so of them in the world now. How do they reach the very top at 35?

They would come earlier and leave later and do more than they are paid and expected of. They think about and learn how their work can be done in a better and more efficient way. They would volunteer to do the work of an employee who is absent. Their eyes and ears are open to know the present and future market trends and reflect on the direction the company should take. Their 'real work' starts when they leave office, learn from the internet and other sources the latest developments in their line of work, search for innovative ideas, how to cut costs and increase efficiency.

They start taking interest in every department – sales, production, accounting, finance, human resource, R&D and study the functions of each in detail sacrificing their free time and pleasures of idling with friends or watching TV. These give them more breadth and prepare them for larger responsibilities. When there is a meeting they give more relevant suggestions and the owners will note in their minds, 'here is the leader for tomorrow.' Promotions would be quick to come by and they become CEOs at 35 or before.

Contrast this with employees, including professionally employed people, who do their work perfunctorily for the pay. Public sector employees' jobs are assured regardless of their work efficiency (there is no evaluation) in many of the emerging economies. They do the bare minimum just to retain the job. There are many of them who will be paid fully for affixing signatures in the attendance register once in a week or once in 2 weeks! A colossal waste of the wealth of the state.

There are professionally employed people who read politics and get involved in heated discussions. It is OK to get to know what is going around but to dissipate one's energy in an area they are not connected with at all, defocuses one's mind. They do not get time to update themselves on the latest trends, discoveries and developments nor are they able to apply their minds on what they are engaged in. They pull on perfunctorily just for the pay, contributing less, if not nothing, to the job.

45. Modeling for quick success

Modeling has become the process of recreating excellence. Scientific modeling involves transferring what an expert knows to oneself. We can model any human behaviour by mastering the beliefs, the physiology and the specific thought processes that underlie the skill or behaviour. Through modeling you can replicate the desirable skill or behaviour of any one. What the person has acquired in a long period of time can be appropriated by you in a much shorter time and hence the whole process is accelerated learning.

One has to copy posture, voice patterns, and adopt dress, grooming and motor skills. The copying is done like mimicry without questioning the why of it. The model's thinking strategies are to be explored and assimilated. One should know his thoughts and beliefs in detail. What books he read, what are his views on various subjects, and how he sees his work and what is the nature of his internal communication (self-talk which goes on without one's conscious control).

Richard Bandler, John Grinder and *Anthony Robbins* have adopted successful people's techniques and acquired their capabilities (which the former took years to cultivate) in a very short time. They have detailed the modeling strategies in their works.

One should know the person extremely well in the particular setting. Pick up the pattern of their behaviours at an unconscious level and 'tune in' your motor-skills to theirs or replicate his patterns of muscle movements, physical postures and gestures, and a number of other minute muscle movements without any rationalization and then you can have the same degree of skill or replicate his behaviour in that setting.

Children learn everything by this modeling process. They do not have any expectation or anxiety of the outcome or consequences of their modeling and they succeed at a phenomenal rate. They learn a language from the early developmental environment inclusive of people who speak the language. Modeling is not based on a rational learning system or conscious intervention. The modellee simply models the person blindly to develop the necessary skills, behaviours, motor skills and unconscious processes that the other person has without trying to interpret what they do. You do not try to understand what you want to learn consciously but you simply try to mirror and match the person.

46. Limiting beliefs (that pull you down)

Perhaps the greatest reason that brings in mediocrity or failure into our lives can be traced to one's limiting belief system. It is a mindset wherein you believe that you have certain limits and that your horizon is confined to them. The beliefs one holds to be true make up the fabric of one's experience. The stronger these beliefs the more unshakable they seem and one will keep on finding evidence to support them.

But what most of us do not realize is that the vast majority of our beliefs about us and the world are not in reality true. Beliefs are formed with repeated thoughts and the reason they hold any weight is because we have decided them to be true.

If one believes that his limits have been set by his parents and home that will become the truth. If another thinks that he is not going to make it, he will not.

Ingrained belief patterns and habits can be a bit harder to change. We are so used to them and we almost identify with them. They feel like immovable objects on our path.

'I am not all that capable and I will not succeed in life,' 'I don't have the requisite abilities to become rich or famous,' 'I do not deserve success,' 'I have done so many wrongs and I deserve this ill-treatment,' these beliefs are deeply ingrained, difficult to change and all efforts must be done to change them.

The first step would be to stop identifying with these beliefs and stop seeing yourself conforming to them. Question all the conclusions you have about what you think to be true. The third way is to question the belief itself. Prove through some result of your focused action that the belief is erroneous. To empower a new belief, you need to spend more time to produce more results proving your belief is wrong. When you aspire for a new dream, the hope is quickly overtaken by doubts like: Do I have the right experience, resources, talents, connections? These will basically justify one's inaction and helplessness. Immediately turn off that doubtful voice and become determined to pursue the dream with all your powers. Repeat this for a number of times and the limiting belief will find its own demise. There are many who have done and you can do it too.

47. Emotional intelligence

In today's world, Emotional Intelligence makes all the difference. EI is the ability to identify, assess, and control one's and others' emotions. People with a better EI tend to be good at interpreting, understanding, and acting upon emotions and are quite good at dealing with social or emotional conflicts.

According to Daniel Goleman, EI is:

1. Ability to read one's emotions and recognize their impact on others.
2. Self-management – controlling one's emotions and impulses and adapting them to changing circumstances.
3. Social awareness – the ability to sense, understand, and react to others' emotions appropriately.
4. One's ability to inspire, influences, and develop others and manage conflict.

EI is partly an inborn characteristic and partly a learnt one. One should be aware of one's emotional set up and its impact on others and learn to control it. He should have an awareness of the emotional set-up of those he comes in contact with and know how to get along with him. Without regulating one's feelings and reactions based on it, he/she can never cultivate meaningful relationships at home or at the work place.

As mentioned earlier, *Theodor Roosevelt* feels that the most important single ingredient in the formula of success is how to get along with people. You cannot achieve great success without the help of others and people are more willing to help you if you have built a meaningful relationship. You cannot be victims of the stimuli-response patterns of behaviour (reacting to a situation based on your instinct like animals do as in the experiment of Maslow). We should decide our reactions suitably and consciously, learning to treat the person with respect, no matter who the person is or how he behaved to you.

Empathy is the ability to know the emotional make-up of other people. It is one of the hallmarks of emotional intelligence. You should be able to treat people, colleagues, family members, subordinates and superiors, as per their emotional set-up. If you react angrily to an angry outburst from one of your workers, friends or dear ones, well, you are just like him or them with no control over your emotions and you cannot be a leader and without becoming one there is no way you can succeed. To effectively behave to people you need to be cognizant of their emotional set-up and the 'why' of their behaviour before you react. The proficiency in building and managing relationships networks, social skills, is a crucial characteristic of emotional intelligence.

48. The theory of progress

Why have certain societies progressed and others regressed? Is it race, or religion that set the pace? Has environment a critical role to play? The whites are obviously more developed than the black or the coloured. But achievement is not their monopoly.

Northern America, Northern Europe, Australia, New Zealand, Japan, and Korea are all advanced. What common thread can we discern in these societies that have triggered the engine of progress? Most of them lie in the temperate region—except USA and Australia. But then the original inhabitants of these nations came from temperate zones. Japan and Korea enjoy cooler climates.

Another common denominator is the harsh nature of the geographical setting. Japan, for instance, lacks natural resources. So is Northern Europe. Further, the former is haunted by natural calamities like earthquakes and volcanoes. Food was not easily available and more effort was required to sustain life. They had to work hard, challenge adversities to live and advance.

Extensive sea shores and chances for easy contact with other societies seem to have helped too.

All the non-developed regions—Africa, Greenland, Southern Asia, the South Pacific Islands, and Latin America have extreme climates. When the ambient temperatures are high, the human body tends to rest as work will increase body heat. In the course of millions of years, humans have evolved indolent and less enterprising.

One would notice too that water and food were relatively more aplenty in Southern Asia and Africa. As the soil was more fertile too, food production was easier. These combined with a hot climate resulted in the evolution of a less hardworking, less enterprising nature. (It is altogether another thing that later food and other essentials became scarce as population exploded).

Even their thinking was affected. A very passive philosophy evolved in these geographical setting. The theory of Non-violence, ahimsa, nirvana, rebirth and karma took root in the course of millions of years. They became more inward-looking and sought inner contentment and total detachment.

As people moved from the comparatively cozy climate of the South and settled in the harsher and cooler regions of the North they had to ward off the ambient cool and work hard to produce the essentials of life. Slowly but steadily, they, through their hard work and enterprisingness, laid the foundations for advancement.

49. Scarcity orientation

Scarcity of food has been the rule among the lower species. Even in human history, we find pervasive scarcity in all fronts. Food has been scarce from the very beginning. Even today, in many parts of the world, a number of people are starving. Famine and draught have made people's lives miserable in large areas of Africa and Asia. A World of plenty is an impossible dream for them. No wonder there is a deep seated scarcity orientation that colours the way they see the world.

It is as if they wear scarcity spectacles that distort their vision. They see resources as limited or scarce. In the ancient times, if anyone took more than 'his fare share' of what food was available he would be seen as evil. If he tried to hoard some food for difficult times ahead, that was a greater evil. Even if one produced more than his needs he could not take more than the others or save the surplus.

This could be the reason why so many people still see profit and wealth making as evil. The 'fare share' principle has been handed down from generation to generation. Your own parents have been victims of this. Hence they said, "Don't waste food. There are so many starving today"; "Be careful with money; they do not grow on trees." They often forced you to share your toys with the other kids. They must have often reminded you about being selfish too. They had a mental orientation that no matter what they do, their money hunger could not be satisfied.

The no-solution-orientation acts like a self-actuating expectation. This has strengthened your belief that your unsatisfied money hunger will persist forever. There is a universal thinking that the starving people should be helped by providing them with the survival needs.

Victim mentality may have its origins in the helpless phase of infancy. We are all born as helpless babies totally dependent on our parents for survival. In a poor house all share the pain, poverty and desperation. Most of the neighbourhood could be in abject poverty too. As a result, they develop a helpless mentality. This distorts their vision and influences their lives negatively.

Abundance is the rule of the nature today. Everything is potentially aplenty. Anyone can become wealthy. Even if all of us have become millionaires, there is scope for further enrichment. Whatever we have on this planet originates from solar energy. We have not been able to use even one trillionth of the energy that comes to earth. There is a huge abundance waiting to be appropriated. ௵

50. Why the poor remain poor?

One of two in India is living in poverty. International agencies, donor nations, government, the UNO and the NGOs, have been extending from time to time free medicines, clothes and financial helps to the poor and the sick. There have been consistent efforts to educate them, to reduce population explosion, empower women and to provide employment opportunities. These have not produced the desired results and millions remain illiterate, poor, sick and emaciated.

The external material helps do alleviate hunger and help to remove disease symptoms. But it does not alter the reality. As soon as the helps stop coming, people return to their previous states. Why the efforts in such a massive scale do not improve their lives? Has it got anything to do with their thoughts, beliefs and attitudes? Can external help alter the life of anybody? Well, if external help could change individuals and societies it would have already done so.

A close analysis would reveal their beliefs and thought patterns remain unchanged. And there has been no effort to alter them. They believe in fate, karma and no-solution-inevitability. They think too they are doomed without external help and it is the duty of the society or the government to uplift them. Their thoughts are about poverty, wants and sickness. They fear what they will eat, where they will sleep and what they will put on tomorrow.

Do their thoughts, fears and emotions create the reality? There seems to be a strong co-relation between the two. A hunger project study conducted by *Wisner Erhard* in 1977, has shown that scarcity orientation and victim mentality are at the root of the world hunger.

Hot humid climate has induced indolence and a helpless attitude. Famine, poverty, diseases and plagues led him to believe in Karma or fate. People believe they are tools in the hands of Fate.

Man has today the power to alter it. The core belief system determines one's mental attitude. And efforts to come up emanate from the latter. Man is no more at the mercy of nature or its forces. Medical science has advanced so much that diseases are under control. Industrial revolution has ensured adequate production of goods and services. Agriculture has developed so much that we are able to produce more food than is required. Man has become the master of his life. Anyone can come, shape his destiny the way one wants to and come up to any level. This belief is the primary requisite and starting point.

51. Creating abundance

The Universe is abundant in every way. There is infinite energy for conversion into material things. Learn the principles of creating abundance. Change your present scarce, poor, limited thinking and believe you can create abundance. Repeat this affirmation a few times holding your hands to your chest: "The Universe is absolutely abundant and is always working for me." As you affirm, open your mind and believe you deserve it. The Universal self will eventually change your reality. Reaffirm: "Now I open myself to receive the riches of the Universe" (If negative thoughts creep in, stop them and reaffirm the positive ones and make this a habit). If you feel you deserve abundance, it comes to you. Many are living with scarcity and they become nervous when they want to request abundance. Repeat to you often, "I deserve to have abundance." If you notice, getting worried about receiving a lot, ask the Universe to help you get the deserving feeling. Slowly you will start believing in your ability to take abundance from the abundant Universe.

Examine your life. Identify an area where you need abundance. What is it that you specifically want - Wealth? Happiness? Fame? Decide exactly what you require. If say, you want money; ask yourself, 'What higher qualities this money would bring me? How will I think, and live differently?' Finding the essence of what you want to create by having abundance is the key to having it. Think of ways you have more of these feelings right now. If wealth brings you feelings of well-being, then think of ways you can create it without creating money first. Starting to create these feelings will make you more magnetic to money. Energy follows Thought. You get what you think about. Believe fully you are already having the money you want. Focus your mind like a laser beam. You will be given a plan by your subconscious mind to make wealth. Follow it blindly.

There is a misconception that you earn something by hard work or good deeds. This is a misnomer. It is all vibrations. If you believe you will have it in your mind and in your heart you will have it. Say, you want health. Acknowledge every time you feel healthy, energetic and alive. Ignore the times you feel tired and sick. When you focus on the positive aspects that are already working, you will draw more of the same towards you. Whatever is the area of abundance you want, learn to be positive. They draw to you more of what you desire.

Acknowledge and appreciate abundance already experienced. Spend some time every day for quiet reflection and meditation on what you desire. If thoughts of scarcity creep in, change them into thoughts of abundance. Repeat the relevant words, and as described with laser beam concentration.

52. Traits of successful people

Successful people are more made than born. Those who advocated the trait theory believed leaders are born with a certain set of characteristics, this is now generally discredited. Anyone can become a leader or successful from any background.

But there are a number of traits common to all successful people. They are generally ambitious, have a vision and do not dabble in everything. They concentrate on their work or area of interest for more than 12-14 hours a day. They do not leave something they started mid-way but carry it on and until completion. They generally seize any opportunity when it comes. They have a lot of setbacks and failures (like all of us) which do not dispirit them. Instead, they take them as challenges and learn lessons from them. These failures do not bother them a lot in their walk towards their goals. They fight back adversities and take responsibility for whatever happens in their lives. They do more than they are paid for or go the extra mile in whatever profession they are in. They do not waste their time and are fruitfully engaged almost always. They are positive people with a pronounced positive attitude. They generally expect positive results. They are generally willing to help others and feel empathy towards those they deal with. Perhaps what makes them successful is their ability to control their emotions and react to others understanding their emotional set-up. Love for their dear ones generally drives them on. They are generally meticulous in their dressing and grooming. They are in a peak state of body physiology and are brisk in their movements.

Well we cannot be all at the top of the tree, but we can rise to a branch by focusing on what we are good at. ☺☺

53. Genetic permutations and combinations

There are a lot of genetic and early childhood variables which influence our lives. Some of us are more gifted with a better grey matter (with its good structure), good biology and good physique. IQ can be high, medium, low or anywhere in between. Similarly, one's EQ varies too. These two together make or break anyone. And we have hardly any control over the inheritance or development of these two most important variables. How many are born with the physical endowments of *Aiswarya Rai, Brad Pitt, Jhon Travolta, Elizabeth Taylor*, and the like. Think about those who are blind, deaf and mute, crippled, psychotic, and mentally retarded and imbeciles.

There are those who are born kings (like *Prince Charles* or the *Nehru descendants*) and millionaires. The children of rich nations like Belgium, USA and other developed nations are born into prosperity. Children of countries like Somalia are born into abject poverty, malnutrition, diseases and death. What did the kids do to inherit abundance, prosperity and an assured future? What crime did the hapless ones born into misery do? Nothing. The accidence of their birth determine their childhood, whether they will die or survive, whether they will wallow in wants or lead a prosperous life.

Thoughtful parents groom their children so that they will succeed in later life and there so those many who do not even take care of their basic needs to survive. Many parents quarrel always and make life in the family a hell. Naturally, these children are in an obvious disadvantage as they develop more inferiority complex, insecurity, anxiety and sometimes self hate. And these traits cannot be easily erased. Can a child born with a low IQ in a strife torn family unloved and unwanted succeed in later life? The chances are low although theoretically one can say yes.

You are better. You have a functional rain (the most crucial aspect), have sufficient education, adequate means of livelihood and you are better than millions of others. Be grateful to your luckier combination and make the best of whatever you have. ☺☺

54. More the failures greater the chance to succeed

Look at the politicians who fail in a general election. They have had devoted a lot of time planning and working for months or years spending their resources. Failure does not discourage them a bit; they take it in their stride and they start scheming for the next event. They analyze their mistakes and shortfalls and take corrective steps and move on; they never give in. They resurrect and win handsomely in a short while. *Mrs. Gandhi* the Indian PM, was defeated in the 1977 general elections and her party was routed. She was arrested by the ruling coalition and put in jail. But she plotted her come back, worked day and night and she won the next general election. In about three years she was the PM again.

They never succumb to despair or frustration even for a minute. This is a great lesson we have to learn from them. They find opportunities in everything, including defeats. It is known to all of us how Edison won after 10,000 failures. Lincoln conquered defeat after defeat which haunted his life throughout and eventually became the president of the United States.

Demosthenes had stammering; he overcame the affliction with years of persistent efforts (he practiced speaking with a pebble under his tongue). He is acclaimed to be the greatest orator ever lived. Narasimha Rao wanted to be the Indian Prime minister. The Nehru clan was so overbearing and the position of PM was appropriated naturally by them. He had to wait and wait serving as a minister in the Indira and Rajiv cabinets. He eventually became the PM after the assassination of Rajiv Gandhi and that too without a majority for his own party.

It is known to all how Helen sans eyes, ears and speech became one of the greatest ladies ever lived. The spider in the story had a number of falls but succeeded. More the failures you are given to endure, greater is the chance you get what you want.

55. Developing self-confidence

Without being confident you cannot even attempt to succeed.

There is no magic to shred off your diffidence. But there are certain steps which might be of help to develop self-esteem.

1. "Do it now" is an old principle. Do not postpone things; finish today's work today itself. If there is a lot of things to do, make a priority list and do the most urgent ones today and the rest the next day.
2. Save some money from whatever you earn and let it grow in the bank. Having something in there gives a feeling of confidence. On the other hand, if you have to borrow from someone, it will erode your confidence.
3. Do a small help a day to a stranger without expecting anything in return. It can be helping a blind cross the road, giving a little money to someone you do not know, consoling an aggrieved friend, removing a thistle or a boulder from the road (so that someone will not be hurt) or helping a stranger who is in real trouble.
4. Try to think, say and do good always as a principle. When you engage in rumor mongering or intentionally telling lies, you are eroding your own self-worth feelings.
5. Do not entertain guilt. We have all done a number of wrong things in the past when we were young or immature. There could be many reasons; many of them were well beyond our control, there could have been adverse home and environmental influences too. There is no point in crying over what has already happened. Forget the past. Learn lessons from them and move on. But do not repeat the same mistakes again. There is no need to feel guilty about anything. The only sin in the world is harming or paining another person.
6. Always be smartly dressed and groomed. Prefer designer ware. Go in for dresses which suites your complexion and appearance. There is no point in going after fashion or what others like. Take care of personal hygiene and let everything you put on be well-thought about and chosen consciously.
7. Try to do more than you are paid for. "Go the extra mile." Your extra work will never go waste. The Universe will reward you a hundredfold. And it will boost your self-esteem hundredfold. Slowly you will start feeling you are a good person.
8. Utilize your free time constructively and ensure you do not remain at the bottom for long.

9. Keep your strengths always highlighted in your mind and downplay weakness. Make a list of all your good points and go through the list often.
10. Become fit and healthy. Your weight should be ideal or as per your Body Mass Index. Eat less, exercise well, and keep yourself fit. A clumsy person cannot feel confident easily.
11. Maintain peak state body physiology. Keep a confident posture. Sit, stand, and walk erect. Let your movements be brisk. Wrong body postures and lethargic moves will make your mind lethargic too.
12. Make sure of some small successes every day. It can be advancing towards your goal by whatever small fraction, taking a positive step towards self-confidence or updating yourself in your chosen field. Even a decision to use your free time purposefully is a 'win'.
13. Expect setbacks all the time. Remember, without fighting adversities or failures no one has gone up.
14. Try to keep your dear ones always happy. Spend quality time with your family and kids. Sacrifice something or the other so that they are happier.
15. Prefer positive minded friends and avoid negative or pessimistic ones. Friends can make or break you.
16. Keep your focus on your goals. Let them guide you like the North Star and have a moral code to guide your actions.

56. Revolutionary selling

Selling has entered a new epoch of non-conventional methods; the old script is simply outdated. There is a new set of rules, approaches and tools. Today, more sales calls may not necessarily result in greater sales. More business can be ensured with fewer calls. Pressuring the clients or applying closing techniques may not necessarily bring in results.

You have to reinvent yourself from a dreaded sales person to a trusted advisor and earn respect. There is a whole new set of rules, approaches and tools. Honesty, deep knowledge and common sense are more effective. There is no headache of innumerable reminders or incessant follow ups. You do not have to talk all the time. You do not have to be an unwanted guest. You can have honest conversations and behave like a thorough professional.

Position yourself as an expert and not as a salesman. Aim at a life time relationship starting from the very beginning. Become a problem solver of the client in everything and give impeccable after-sales service.

Let your prospects know you through referrals and a well designed professional web site giving every detail. Through proper questions, get into his intimate zones. Know the type of your customer-director (shows ego), socializer (expresses feelings), thinker (why do you ask questions?), relator (who asks to talk about you) and handle each one accordingly.

But with all these, the golden rules: have excitement and a good attitude, have a thorough business knowledge, focus on the top 20% interested customers, do follow up and concentrate on after sales are all still applicable and essential. Be in your best body language dress and groom well. Be relaxed to sell more. Be confident before your customer. If you get a 'no' ask why, why not? After a no, do not beat yourself. Fill your mind with your successes and forget the failure. It is his problem not yours. Keep your excitement and enthusiasm throughout. Improve your sales behaviour through learning, listening, experiencing. Talk only good about your competitors, and take every complaint as a great opportunity to build up the reputation of the company.

Identify the pain if he does not buy and the pleasure if he does. Produce testimonials from people the customer knows. Give full attention, never displease him, and follow up until you win. Do not give promises you cannot (or do not intend to) keep up. Let your behaviour be professional all the time and never let it slip down to a personal level. They want professional services from you all the time before or after the sales. You should always fulfill promises made and do more.

57. Move briskly to succeed

Body and mind are interconnected; body physiology — the way you stand, sit, walk, talk, look, hold your head, chest and do gestures reveal your mental state. The most efficient body physiology – brisk and definite body postures, walking, looking and talking bring in success. A more confident state can be induced by being erect, having an open body posture and by moving briskly.

On the other hand, by dropping shoulders, looking down, breathing shallow and muttering negative things infernally, a sad state would be induced. By changing the physical state, mental state can be altered and the reverse is true too. Sadness, diffidence, sorrow or failure makes one look down, drop shoulders, breathe shallow, and sit, stand like a defeated one.

There is a recent thinking that success implies moving more. The relation between moving briskly always and succeeding is well established. The more and brisker your movement the greater your success. Observe top level executives; they all move briskly around, sit and walk in their peak state body physiology. *Barak Obama* has always been in his peak state body physiology. And he became supremely self-confident and defeated a white lady to become the US president.

One will have an energetic and enthusiastic mind if one keeps her body always in a peak state and move briskly. Highly successful executives are always more energetic and more brisk in everything they do than the slow and lethargic ones. Death comes when movement stops. As old age advances you see people on decrepitude. They do not move and every organ starts to die.

In my seminars, I used to give this challenge to the participants: "there is a simple secret to succeed: move and walk briskly always." Presuming it is very simple they start from the next day in right earnest. But in a day or two they all return to their old ways. You see, it is not that simple or easy. You need a bulldog determination as a new habit is to be established by following the new pattern uninterruptedly for at least one and half months. Once you do, you feel you more important and confident. Lethargy and slowness will eventually make you a good for nothing guy. Change the way you hold and move your body and change your destiny. ☺☺

58. Fast to become healthy

Today there are very few who are willing to forgo food; on the contrary we all want to eat more. Even the sick do not abstain from dining; there is a misconceived notion that eating helps body recover. It does not; it only harms. We have to learn from animals which totally fast when they are sick.

Parents try to force-feed children when they are sick; wives do the same to their husbands especially if they are newly-wed. Abstaining from food during sickness is deemed incorrect by almost all of us: we have to fast or take little while we are indisposed so that the body energy could be channelized for curing. Many are aware of the fact that overeating is harmful but very few know that fasting and eating less is good for health. Fasting is, perhaps, the best medicine ever.

Fast occasionally for a day; if that is uncomfortable skip lunch or dinner. Skip the snacks in between and reduce your intake. It has been conclusively proven that if our calorie intake is limited to 1200 per day (our average calorie intake is above 2500 or more) we will live much more and that too healthily. Now the choice is yours. Eat less and enjoy health and longevity or eat sumptuously to your heart's content (with good servings of fatty and fried stuff) and become sick and cut short your life.

The past is past and done with. How you have lived hardly matters. The now and the future is that which counts. Decide at this moment to reduce your intake, fast occasionally and enjoy health. Eat only when you are really hungry and not because it is lunch or dinner time. Decide to take more fibrous food and water with deep coloured fruits and vegetables; less sugar, salt and alcohol. If this effort is combined with exercises you are going to be super-fit.

59. Life just begins now

Your life begins right now. The past is over and done with. The future stretches out ahead of you in myriad forms. You take flight now and soar up in the horizon with your dreams acting as a beacon to guide you.

This should be your desire. Every day you repeat this: "My life begins today. I have lived years but I feel I am starting my life right now like a kid. I do feel that my real life lies ahead with a bright future where I will conquer new territories and achieve new goals. Physically and mentally I feel afresh, I am just about to begin my new life. The past is a flicker and what is going to unfold is a full life. Everything lies ahead; everything just begins."

We all know that present moment is always new. The new is constantly shedding the old. Life works through this process. A spring that stops replenishing its new water soon turns dank and sour. If anything in life fails to shed the old, it quickly stagnates. Every one of us must aspire for a new life. I am not mentioning the natural life process mentioned above. I talk about a new life that just begins like that of a teenager.

The real danger lies when you feel life is getting over, that the good old days have passed by. It is when you feel you are now past your prime and that what lie ahead is the slanting rays and long shadows.

Have you lost the curiosity and the agility of a child? Is your mind dull and the body heavy? Have your joints become stiff, your muscles tight and your mind set in a rut? If yes, you can undo or refresh them. Go to the gym, start exercising. Do not sit and idle away your time. Be purposefully engaged and be on the move always. Control your diet, eat less and regain your shape. Make your memory work through crossword or brain puzzles, take care in grooming, and be interested in people of the opposite sex. You can again become like a teen. You can have the mind of a child-well if that is what you want. If you feel you are old you are. If you feel your life is finished it is.

60. Picture your dream into reality

The great Roman emperor, *Marcus Aurelius* wrote: 'our life is what our thoughts make it.' The famous psychologist *William James* of Harvard stated thus: 'belief (intense mental picture) creates the actual fact.'

If you can picture clearly and vividly and constantly what you want to be, after say, 15 years you are definitely going to become that.

Your persistent thoughts and the accompanying mental pictures control your life and determine your future. Keep picturing and thinking of what you want and you are certainly going to become that. If your dominant thoughts are of failure you will constantly play in your mind a movie of failure and you will end up as a big failure. If your dominant thoughts are of success you will reap success. Your life will be consistent with what you mentally picture constantly. But if your mental pictures are not consistent, your subconscious mind will have no direction and it will have to group in the dark in guiding your life.

To become what you want to be, frequently picture yourself what you want to become. When you mentally picture the kind of person you want to become, place no limit on your mental picture. You will become whatever you consistently picture in your mind. The all-powerful subconscious mind does not place any limit on what you can become. Remember the subconscious mind connects the limited mind to the infinite Universe and its powerhouses.

One's mental picture becomes one's future. As the rich see more wealth mentally they become richer. The poor sees poverty, wants and diseases all the time in their inner eye and they become poorer and sicker. Your mental pictures provide motivational guidance and condition your attitudes so that you will act in a guided manner to achieve the objectives you hold in your continuous and persistent thoughts. You become what you repeatedly and intensely picture.

As your subconscious mind is being bombarded with countless stimuli, impulses, memory recalls and responses, it is rather a difficult task to keep the required thoughts and pictures down there. Further, you cannot impress your subconscious with a weak, vague, infrequent, indifferent, indistinct mental picture. You have to constantly hold a self image of the person you want to eventually become so that it is etched indelibly into the screen of your mind. You have to intensify the mental picture so that it will be your constant dominant thought and all your principal thinking will relate directly or indirectly to it.

Your subconscious mind will produce what you want in direct proportion to the intensity and frequency of the mental pictures. You can emphasize with words what you are picturing. Repeat your life goal in three or four words very forcefully hundreds or thousands of times at every opportunity.

61. Gain instant courage to face a difficult situation

Imagine you have to meet the dreaded boss tomorrow. The very thought of meeting him sends a shiver through your spine. How can you gain enough confidence at the moment? Do the exercise below and become instantly courageous.

Sit erect in a chair and breathe in and out a few times deeply and slowly. As you exhale, feel every cell of your body getting relaxed, feel your entire body getting quiet and settled. Start counting slowly from ten to one and as you count down feel you are more quite, settled and relaxed.

Now bring to your mind a very confident experience or a winning situation of your life. Go through it in full detail. See every sight you had seen in full colour and with more intensity very close to you. Hear every sound amplified and brought nearer to your mind. Feel the same way you had felt then more intensely. You body physiology will change immediately. Your head will be held straight and shoulders drawn. Your breathing will become deeper and slower. Start experiencing the good feeling and savour a resurgent confidence. As you reach its peak or when you feel really confident and courageous, tighten both your fists. You now open them in a jerk saying "yes" simultaneously. Feel a new surge of courage invigorating every cell of your body.

Immediately, start breathing and exhaling deeply and slowly. Count from 10 to 1 as before and bring the winning situation into your imagination. Savour the whole experience and hear the sounds magnified, sights made in colour and nearer to your mind and feel the whole thing precisely as you had felt. At the peak of the confidence you feel, tighten your fists and say, "yes" and suddenly open them. Make sure you to close the fists and to open them and say "yes" exactly as you same way did before.

Do these five or six times. Hear, see and feel the experience, tighten fists, and say "yes" when you open them in identical ways, each time savouring the new surge of courage through your sinews. The next day, say you have to meet your boss or your girl friend. You simply tighten your fists and say yes and you will feel a new surge of confidence. Now go and meet your dreaded boss or face the interview or meet your girl friend.

62. If you believe in longevity, accident is not possible

If you fully believe you will have a long and healthy life, can an accident or natural calamity defeat it?

In all probability, no. Your brain, the subconscious part of it, which is in absolute harmony with the Universal Intelligence, will honour your beliefs. But how? Will you escape an earth-quake that hits your area? Certainly, if your belief in longevity is strong enough. Your subconscious mind which is, as already mentioned, in communion with the universal mind, will protect you. It will be seeking ways to save you. Being warned of the impending danger, it would ask you beforehand to go to another place on business or on a sightseeing trip or on some other pretext. If a quake happens in the night it would awake you up early enough and command you to go out and take shelter. At the worst, you would be among the survivors.

Will you die in a plane crash? I think it is absolutely improbable. You will not be able to avert the crash. The forces involved, gravity of the earth and the weight of the aircraft are too big for your thought energy to stop or control. But your subconscious mind which is in 'tune' with the Universal mind would have asked you not to book a seat in the doomed aircraft. You would go earlier or later. If you happened to be in it by some unknown reason (very improbable) there would be little chance for your survival. If the engine failed in midair gravity would certainly pull it down. When that happens everyone dies. But if there is a survivor it would be you!

If you desire and expect health and longevity with all your mind and with all your heart there is almost no chance of running into an accident or succumbing to a disease. It will make you more cautious in everything. You will take precautions in driving. You will not drive after drinking and you will be very careful in night driving and overtaking. You would be more alert about your safety in everything even without your knowledge. The subconscious mind becomes ever vigilant and makes you precautious all the time. Accidents simply do not happen.

When you walk or jog, you would take extra precautions too. You will walk away from the carriageway so that no running vehicle can brace you. Your eyes and ears would be always alert to ensure your safety.

Those who think and worry about illnesses only get sick. With your belief, your subconscious mind creates an invisible ring of protection around you all the time. Those who pursue big goals have no time to be worried about sickness and they are generally healthier. You will not be even led to situations where you will be infected with the HIV, Hepatitis B or any such deadly virus. There comes a guardian angel sort of thing around you all the time.

63. Focus........Focus

Why do some people achieve the same results in 30 hours for which others take 45 or more? It is simply attention. Result is directly proportional to focus.

The more the thinking and actions you do in pursuit of your goals the more the success you experience. When you start focusing on a task, your mind starts to offload solutions, procedure and everything required to complete the task. When your focus is distracted, you do not get the desired result.

Apple succeeded in a great measure simply because it focused on a few products and ignored so many other great ideas. It is simple to succeed in life: have a clear mission and focus on it constantly. Get continued focus and clear success. Controlling the time at hand is a necessary tool to learn to focus.

Most of us live as if we have all the time in the world. We have very limited time. If we do a time analysis from the moment we wake up to that we retire we would find a number of wasted or idling hours.

We all have the same 24 hours each day. What makes a successful person different from a mediocre one is the way each spends these 24 hours. Do not waste this precious commodity by indulging in the trivial. Many of us just do the emergencies and simply 'fill in' the rest of the day. We postpone actions required to get our aims to a later day which never comes. When the grey twilight begins to fall we conveniently forget about these goals we had cherished to achieve.

To know what things are to be done we should clearly have a concept of what we need not do at all. Concentrate your time only for those activates that will advance you to your mission.

Peter Trucker says, "There is nothing as useless as doing efficiently what should not be done at all."

Remember what *Confucius* said long back, "if you chase two rabbits you catch neither."

You can catch one by focusing on one. The secret of success is focus.

64. Getting what you want

There is a procession of thoughts and pictures passing through your mind continuously. Unless you consciously control the flow of thoughts and pictures, unwanted thoughts and pictures will fill the mental space and your subconscious mind will be all at a loss in guiding you. These uncontrolled thoughts and pictures can be pleasant day-dreams or worry, anxiety, resentment, hatred, emotional experiences or situations. The negative thoughts and pictures will become the source of subconscious guidance with disastrous consequences.

It is important that you learn to streamline your thought process. Normally an average human has 70,000 thoughts passing through his mind in quick succession. If more than 35,000 thoughts are on a single aim for a considerable period, it will be translated into reality. It is enough to keep your mind focused on the goals you have set for more than half the time you are awake or for about 8 hours.

How to control this uncontrolled flow of thoughts and pictures?

Relax your body with a few deep breaths, close your eyes and black out all pictures from your mind and fill your mental screen with darkness until your mind is relaxed. Calmly but deliberately replace the temporary darkness with bright and intense mental pictures of what you want to become.

Your subconscious is not impressed with the importance of attaining your life goal more than you care. You have to constantly hold a self-image of the person you want to eventually become so that it is etched indelibly into the screen of your mind. You have to intensify the mental picture so that it will be your constant dominant thought and all your principal thinking will relate directly or indirectly to it. You can emphasize with words what you are imagining. Repeat your life goal in three or four words very forcefully hundreds or thousands of times at every opportunity.

Suppose you want to become a renowned author you can coin the rods, 'publish famous books' or if you want to be rich, say 'make a billion' often forcefully. Be excited about what you say as the subconscious mind picks up the vibrations of thought which are emotionalized. Constantly repeat your coined words in 1-2 seconds excitedly and emphatically accompanied with vivid, colourful mental pictures at least 2000 times during a day. It will be helpful to think about why you want to be successful or rich or anything else and what will you do with the riches you accumulate or the fame you get. The 'why' of your goal will emotionalize it and pass it over to the subconscious mind more forcefully. If you constantly flood the subconscious mind with the mental pictures of you succeeding it will translate your thoughts into reality.

65. These balancing rocks have lived millions for years

There are many of us, including me, who feel that we have been lucky enough to have been born. We are now living in the most advanced civilization (compared to the past and not to the future). We are lucky to marvel at this beautiful world and the most beautiful experience of life. For how long? For a fleeting second! When the curtain falls everything is over. Darkness will prevail forever. Was it better to have had been in the darkness forever? There was no need for a flicker of light for a second.

May be for time, death and birth are all like the joy and sadness we feel in this fleeting second.

The sands we tread on live for millenniums. Those balancing rocks have existed for billions of years. This giant Banyan tree has seen the smile and sighs of so many generations of humans. Its roots have been wetted by the tears of so many generations. It has witnessed the wooing of so many couples and later their great grand children's romance. It is standing there very strong now to witness the courtship of the 21st century teenagers in a unique way. Much more change is yet to come. The mountain over there have witnessed so many such trees come and go. The earth has been spinning around the sun for more than 4 billion years now. And it goes strong even now without any considerable change at all in the speed of spinning or the time taken to go around.

Irrespective of what we experience now, it is going to be pitch darkness without the faintest glow of light from anywhere after a short while. Just eternal darkness will surround us all. Darkness will become the only reality.

Let your profession and goals harmonize with your inner you. Listen to the still voice, the inner guide within. Let your inner instincts and the reservoir of intuition guide you in your choices. As a rule, by the time you are in your early twenties you will know what work or profession you enjoy, what harmonizes with your inner self.

66. You can succeed too

Success is not a mystery; it is the result of the application of a number of known principles. Failure results when one makes same mistakes over and over.

All successful people have definite time-bound goals and their entire energy is pivoted around efforts to achieve them. Or all successful people excel in their chosen field. They work for 13-14-16 hours a day. But they do not feel like working; it all plays and work.

True success can also be a measure of how many times we bounce back when we fall down. It need not always be 'how high we go'. Every success story is also a story of great failure. Abraham Lincoln failed in almost everything he attempted except a few like the presidential election in which he was elected to the highest office of the land. Edison success failure ratio is 1:10,000!

Everyone cannot be truly great; ordinary people become successful by doing whatever they do in a great way. They always do more than they are paid for and success comes as a reward for their extra work.

Successful people always believe they will succeed. Even in the depths of failure they see descending lifts to take them high. All successful people have great desires to come up in life. In fact that is the starting point. Everyone has desires. But why so very few only succeed? The successful ones make the desires intense, a red-heat of desire. The intensity of their desires forces the universal forces to propel them up.

We all want to win, but very few of us are prepared to pay the price to win. We reach a position according to our input. The greater the price paid the greater the reward or output. As *Napoleon Hill* says, "There is no principle called something for nothing. You get that which you paid for." Those who chose to drift and become easy-going and waste their free time will never reach anywhere.

Michelangelo once said, "If people knew how hard I had to work to gain mastery, it wouldn't seem wonderful at all." Success is not something that you get just like that. It takes a lot of thinking, planning, and hard work. It is not luck or good fortune. The harder one works the luckier he gets.

Some people never try at all because they are afraid of losing. Well, if you never try you may not fail but you will never succeed too. Prosperity and riches success of any kind are the results of painstaking and sweating. Those who want to succeed take calculated risks.

Will you be successful? Check this out: How many hours a day are you willing to work for what you want in life? 15-16 hours for a prolonged period? You are certainly on your way to success.

Only the losers will think that life is unfair. Once after a concert, a participant from the audience came unto a great musician. He said, "I would give my life to play the way you do." The musician replied, "I did."

You do not have to be highly intelligent or have high academic qualifications to succeed. You only need to have a disposition to do more than required of you. Even small achievements require a lot of focused thought and work. Have you ever thought, 'why highly educated and highly qualified ones fail in life?' They do not apply whatever they know in a focused way and they do not want to do more than required of them.

67. Predict your future by creating it

Our dreams, thoughts and the consequent actions determine our present and future. How and what we choose, upon what we focus, concentrate or direct our attention, and where we spend our emotional energies, these precisely determine what we will attract.

The physical mechanism that manifests our dreams is important too. There is an absolute connection between our thoughts, feelings, concentration or focus and our present and future. Our thoughts define what is to be and our feelings and emotions provide the energy. They help manifest the reality. The greater the depth of our emotions, the greater is the likelihood of that reality predominating over others.

There is a time buffer in which we must maintain our thoughts for their manifestation. It allows us time to further define our vision, make adjustments as we collect data and determine the advisability of each aspect of our dream.

The present common belief that we must, through hard work or good deeds, earn whatever benefit that comes to us is fundamentally wrong. Earning is all contained in vibrations and thoughts. If you think you must earn a reward, then you will have to. But if you believe fully you already have it, you will soon have it.

"Imagination is the most powerful force,' said *Einstein*. 'As a man thinks so is he,' says *Bible*. You are the cause for everything that happens in your life—whether you are conscious of it or not. The physical world is an effect and not a cause. Everyone today knows that our minds affect matter. You cannot achieve anything by manipulating the effect; Instead, look to change your thoughts, the real cause. You see what you believe and do not believe what you see.

68. Down with dowry!

Man and woman are on an equal footing in the developed nations and marriage is decided by the boy and the girl and conducted the way they want. Parents are invited for the function and there is no dowry whatsoever. They decide their life after the marriage and the two families just keep away from their lives.

In the developing world: oppression begins from the time a girl is born. Girls of East and North Africa are even subjected to female genital mutilation depriving them of sexual pleasures once and for all. There are girls kidnapped and raped to force them into marriage. Girls can be surrendered as a sex slave to patch up with an enemy family. Bride burning, stoning to death, acid attacks and divorces at the will of the husband are all very common.

In most of the Arab world and the African continent, bride's money (called lobola in Africa) is to be given by the groom to the brides' parents. But this does not in any way mitigate her suffering or the ill-treatment meted out to her. The money is appropriated by the girl's father and she becomes a purchased commodity or personal property with no right whatsoever.

Men and women are created equal by nature, their intelligence levels are the same. Man is physically stronger, but women generally are more patient and they have a better EQ. In the evolutionary history, men and women have been assigned different and distinct roles vital for the survival of the species and accordingly they evolved. Women deserve a dignified life with self-respect.

But in India, trouble for a girl begins from the moment of birth. A huge dowry is to be arranged and she is considered inconsequential: boys are the breadwinners and the torch bearers of the family. The amount of dowry depends on the education, job and family status of the boy. There is a lot of bargaining and it is like the sale of a commodity. In certain places apart from the huge amount, other items like furniture, cattle, household utensils and cars have to be handed over. It all depends on the final agreements between the elders of the two families. The buyer ends up getting the commodity and the bargained price.

Even after all the transactions are completed and the girl transferred to the groom's house, she has to bear a lot of pressure from the in-laws to persuade her parents to give more. If the dowry is incomplete, real tragedy awaits her. The in-laws try persuasion before they start the real torture. In some cases she will be killed or burnt which will pave the way for a new marriage and a substantial new dowry. The in-laws will manage to prove she committed suicide: anything is possible here with money and influence. Even after a number of years of 'married' life she is subjected to physical torture, unrewarded hard work, beating, abuse, and all sorts of physical and mental oppression.

Statistics show that in India, about 20,000 brides are killed every 3 years by the in-laws for providing dowries deemed insufficient by the in-laws. Dowry was outlawed in 1961. Still the practice is widespread among all the communities of India. If the dowry is insufficient or not fully paid up, the bride's life will be horrendous.

The Problem can be solved if the youth of India, Islamic world and Africa could accept that:

1. Boys and girls are equal in every way and are to be treated at par.
2. Families should give equal opportunity for education and employment to girls and boys with equal rights for parents' wealth.
3. Dowry or bride's money will not be taken or given.
4. Girls have every right a boy is entitled to including the right to divorce.
5. Vow to stop engaging in eve-teasing or oppression of any sort.

69. Nature is indifferent to man

Nature has ever been indifferent to the survival of any species. Nature has been indifferent to man. It does not bother whether man lives or dies, prospers or becomes poor. From the pre-historic times, earth quakes have devastated him, Volcanoes have spewed out mountains of fire and millions have been killed in the process. Hurricanes, storms, floods, famines, epidemics have all played havoc on human life. Cholera, tuberculosis, malaria, plaques of various kinds has decimated his numbers. But reproduction has been on such a massive scale that he has survived. In a single plague of Europe in the nineteenth century alone, a quarter of the entire population of Europe perished. With the advancement of medicine, man has been able to survive better and improve his life-span. Survival of a human child is no more left to chance. But still, new viruses are evolving like the HIV and they threaten his very existence here. Nature does not bother whether man lives here or not. Nature goes on as per the gravitational, physical and chemical laws of matter. Unaware of the existence of humans. It has been cruel to man in every way.

Still, man has risen from his mammalian ancestors to the pinnacles of civilization we experience today.

70. Life in the 22nd century

'How will be life, its culture and values in the 22nd century?' What will all be the innovative technologies? How will it be different from the present one? No one can certainly predict them.

According to the UN Population Bureau, life expectancy in 2200, will be around 100 for developed countries and the world population will be about 22.8 billion. In the advanced nations, emphasize will probably be on super-intelligent and disease free kids. Genetic engineering would remove all traits of a host of genetically transmitted afflictions. Will man succeed in conquering the ageing process? Will he be at the brink of conquering death? In another century, perhaps, man will decide when he will die.

Organized tours will be frequent to the space and moon and the tourism industry will be more vertical than horizontal. Computer will have a far-reaching influence in our lives. The "computer-modified organism" or robots will probably be used to meet our luxuries and everyday needs.

Imaginative people predict the invention of water-fuelled engines, one of the biggest inventions of all times. It means that the price of water will probably rise and it will contribute to the development of high-technology machines and stronger satellite connections. There could be light-propelled spaceships that can investigate a host of things.

Creating effective immune drugs will be a great leap in the medical field. We are already on the verge of synthesizing successful anti-cancer drugs. Fitness and nutrition will be the fad of the time. A revolution can be expected in the food habits and food production methods. Ready-made foods that will tickle the taste buds of man will replace the traditionally cooked meals.

Little spoken languages and linguistic communities will disappear. English will predominate in the world. Each one of us living then will have the opportunity to speak, write, read, listen to and use English as a means of massive communication. All the other languages will be sidelined.

Family structure will erode and very few women will opt for permanent marriage or child bearing. Marriages of convenience will be more sought after. More will rent wombs or resort to artificial insemination. This is already in vogue: cloning may replace it. But the chances for the latter are less. Nobody wants exact replicas. Diversity will be more attractive. The population will dwindle further in all the advanced countries and those of the poor increase.

The strong ties of family are bound to erode and there will be professional homes to bring up children like we have 'old age homes' now. The gender discrimination is bound to close even in the backward regions.

Will religions have the mad sway which they enjoy now in the less developed nations? There will be a total transformation. More than a quarter of humanity (in the developing nations) will deliver themselves from the clutches of the organized religions. But as the religious roots can be traced to the very beginning of man's evolution, and as human brains are fully programmed into a belief in gods it will take a few more centuries for their total eclipse. But the moment man conquers death, the death of god is certain.

71. Develop your self-esteem

Make an inventory of your assets. Just start writing down right now the good qualities you possess. It could be your IQ, hard working nature, organized ways, ability to make friends, reading/learning habit, honesty, ambition, smartness, care in personal appearance, integrity, ability to connect with others, saving mentality, self-confidence, loving dear ones, pleasing nature, patience, love of details, ability to control emotions, helping nature. Well, mention anything and everything you consider good in you. Your list can go on ....let the list be a little exhaustive. Keep the file open for a few days and ask those who know you well to help you. Once a comprehensive list is prepared, type them out neatly and go through the list everyday once just before sleeping and once just after waking up in the morning.

Should we list down our negatives? After all, 'Knowing thyself' is an old adage. But we will ignore our weak points for the time being. (It is of course good to be aware of things like our hot temper so that we become conscious of losing it thereby we will be able to control the same).

There must have been a lot of past unpleasant experiences in your life just like in anybody else's. We have to learn to throw them away from our minds. Experiences stay put or opt to leave depending on how we entertain them. If we accentuate them they get impressed and they refuse to leave; if we fade them into insignificance they simply disappear.

If you recall an unpleasant past experience in colour, make it black and white and fade it further into a defused sate. See the entire thing far away from your mind. Lower the pitch of the sounds you hear and let them echo from afar. Let the feeling part be made insignificant. Make the whole experience small and then smaller. If it was the size of a football earlier bring it down to the size of a cricket ball and still smaller may be to the size of a pin head. Then you throw it out of your mind. Now it has very little impact on you. The faint defused echoes of something will altogether disappear. Fill the space thus created with a positive experience. Let your mind be filled with powerful experiences enabling you to become more confident.

72. Why are we Christians, Hindus or Moslem?

Have you ever thought why you are a Christian, Buddhist, Sikh, Moslem or Hindu? Is it because you have analyzed every religion threadbare and come to the conclusions that yours is the only true one? Most of us do not attempt to do anything like that. We just believe what we have been taught from our very childhood.

We do not question what has been imparted from day one. That could be the reason why children born to Christian parents become Christians, those born to Hindu parents become Hindus, and Moslem parents Moslem.

There are occasional 'jumps' from one faith to another. This is a universal phenomenon and is not confined to any one in particular. There have been mass conversions too. When the Roman emperor converted to Christianity, the entire subjects had to become Christian. When the Persians conquered India, millions were converted forcibly into Islam. Today also, mass conversions do take place mostly in the developing countries, due to traceable reasons. Even in the advanced nations, conversions happen from one sect to another due to mostly selfish or social motivations and preferences.

But these are exceptions and the vast majority remains steadfast in the religion of their birth. Our childhood brain gets programmed into believing our birth-religion. We do not question its veracity or analyze critically its basic tenets later. We are led to simply continue to believe.

You may believe because you know it is the true religion which you have experienced. But the experience we feel is simply produced by our brain as per our intense belief. The religious experience of a Christian is totally different from that of a Buddhist, Moslem or Hindu.

No religion is better than another one. Every religion has good points. Experiences vary according to one's own beliefs. A true Buddhist does not believe in God. He may not have the experience which a monotheistic religions follower like that of Christianity or Islam has. A communist who is an atheist does not experience God at all. A Hindu believes that the underlying principle of everything in the Universe is one: the Absolute Brahma. God is not separate from the person; God is you. Christians look for a spiritual heaven where they can experience the Almighty God after death, Moslems look for a material heaven. For Buddhists it is Nirvana: the escape from pain and pleasure, cold and heat. The Hindus long for redemption from the birth-rebirth cycle. These tenets are all totally different. Still, people continue to believe what they have been conditioned to believe.

This is applicable to our culture, food and dress habits. We all like our ways of eating, dressing and socializing. Each society has its own peculiar culture and none can say this is a better culture than that or that we are superior/inferior to others.

In the absence of the early childhood programming, how many of us will believe what we do now? We go on as per the software implanted in us from our home environment, religious institutions and culture. And we believe what we believe is true too to the exclusion of all the others. We are compartmentalized which leads to war, communal strife and conflict forgetting we are all brothers and sisters.

73. Secret of a long life from Acacia

Acacia, a mountainous region of Georgia, is famous for longevity. Almost all are centenarians; their average age is 110. This region is heaven-like for those who live in today's air, water and sound polluted cities.

They are active, energetic and hardworking. They respect the old and look forward to becoming 'seniors'. The 'Acacians' do not retire. The young ones' work for more than 12-14 hours. Those who have passed 90, work a few hours less. They are always fruitfully engaged. They live in harmony with nature; songs and dances are an integral part of their lives. And they are, at any age, healthy and happy.

The place is full of hills, valleys and mountains. There is a lot of scope for physical exertion. It is common for them to walk up to 20 miles a day! They climb hills, go down the valleys, swim in fresh waters, cultivate vegetables, fruits and engage in animal husbandry. They eat comparatively less and that too fruits, fresh vegetables, milk products and whole grains. No fast food, no oil, no fried stuff, not much fat, less salt, less sugar and more water.

They ride horses, swim, walk long distances and sleep well. Even those who have crossed 100, believe that they are still young. The society respects 'senior citizens' (above 100). They are still active in the society. Compare this with our stressful, sedentary life-style eating all fast, oily fatty foods! No wonder we become incapacitated earlier and die in youth as diseases overpower our vital organs.

Shall we infer the secrets of a long, healthy life from the Acacians? Exert every day (either through exercises or work), move more, eat less that too fruits and vegetables like spinach, broccoli, carrots and grains; have an active social life and engage oneself in useful work all the time.

74. Let women partake in nation building

The living conditions of women are excellent indicators of the status of the nation. By this yardstick, India is a very backward country. Her 550 million women (less than the number of men due to female infanticide and selective abortion) are still leading a life of utter poverty, illiteracy and neglect in a patriarchal society. One of the causes for persistence of hunger and abject poverty in India is due to the subjugation, marginalization and disempowerment of women. The oppression of women is so much here that Indian women do not even think about equality.

The Indian woman is jobless, hungry and malnourished, poor illiterate, oppressed, anemic and unhealthy. She lives in a poor home with four or five children and an alcoholic and abusive husband. Women suffer from hunger and poverty much more than men and she has the primary responsibility to feed, educate and guide the children. Women are more hungry and malnourished than men as they have to eat at last (even when they are lactating) after ensuring the male members are served. Females get less food and less health care.

Girls get less education (the preference is always for boys), even if sent to school they are pulled back to help the household. Women end up working more hours than men (often more arduous work) and their work goes unrecognized and unpaid. Women who are employed outside have to do the entire household work all by themselves and the males only find fault with what they do.

A guy who marries a girl has to be offered a huge dowry and other valuables as per the pre-agreement of the conditions of the 'sale' of the woman. She is like a commodity sold by her family to his family, the only difference being the sold item has to be offered with a huge amount. A girl is expected to be a virgin before marriage but the boy's past does not matter at all. After marriage, she is generally ill-treated, assaulted and murdered (for bringing fewer dowries) in the groom's household by the husband and in-laws.

Female infanticides and selective abortions are common too. The constitution of India guarantees equality but under the prevailing patriarchal society and its norms, women are powerless to decide their life or the number of children they want, whom they will marry or what they will do.

Women are traditionally responsible for the welfare of their families but excessive poverty (more than one in two of all women is under extreme poverty) make them helpless. Without family planning measures she delivers a number of children, many of whom die an early death adding to her misery and she herself may die at childbirth.

Women are confined within the four walls of the house unable to have a meaningful life, or contribute to the development of the society and family as a whole. There may be exceptions to this in the urban areas but as a whole it holds good. The plight of women and their backwardness could be the single most reason for the underdevelopment of India. ◎◎

75. You alone are responsible for your life

Does any help come from above? Not for the poor. They are in pain and poverty all the time. One in 4 in India get only Rs.11 or less a day! When I write these words there are dozens of children who are dying without food and water. May be in Somalia, may be in India or Ethiopia or Eritrea. There are thousands of infants who die out of mal-nutrition and sickness each day. When a tsunami occurred a few years back, a few hundred thousand people, mostly poor ones living along the costs perished in a moment. Earthquakes, floods and hurricanes kill thousands every year.

Why are they sent down putting an end to all the dreams the victims have so painstakingly built up? Of all the children born into this world a vast majority of them died before the age of 10 until the twentieth century. It was in the 19th and 20th centuries that man developed medical science and preventive medicine. There was no cure for any contagious disease until then and entire society used to be wiped out in plague or in epidemic.

Nature is indifferent to man. It does not bother whether you are alive or dead whether you are poor or rich, healthy or sick. If you win it is good for you. If you fail you suffer alone.

Pain and suffering has been the reality ever since man's appearance on this planet. It continues even today, at a lesser degree as man has advanced in many fields now. There has been no help coming from above in any way. If man tries hard he can survive, prolong his life or succeed. Otherwise, he will be in abject poverty and sickness until death. We are totally responsible for what we are and what we will be.

Accepting misery and pain as god-sent (terming them karma or destiny) is a sure recipe for utter failure. You are the only one who can overcome your poverty, backwardness and failures. If you do not take responsibility for your life no one else will and it is almost certain you are going to be miserable. The world is not interested whether you were born poor, whether you were not educated or whether you grew up diffident with inferiority or other complexes. The world will be with you only if you are a success in life.

76. Change your map to change your destiny

The world looks quite rich, interesting and alright for many of us but it is dull, empty and cruel to many others. All the time the world is the same. The difference comes from the way we perceive it. Our internal maps, our personality and attitude makes the same world look diverse and opposite.

If you want to see opposition you will see it, if you want opportunities you will discover them too. It is all in your minds. The same person appears good to some, bad to others and neutral to still others.

Author *Herb Cohen* says, 'we see things as we are.' You see the map out there as per your internal map. If you do not like a person, in all probability you will be suspicious of anything he does. You may even find fault with whatever he does. If, on the other hand you like another one, you will like whatever he does. It is the way various individuals perceive one that makes the whole difference. What you see mainly depends on what you look for. There are a few who complain roses have thorns and there are so many others who adorn the colour, fragrance and beauty of the flower.

How you see things on the outside will very much depend upon how you are on the inside. Anything facing us is not as important as our attitude towards it. You change your attitude and the things changes within moments. When you are positioned correctly, right opportunity presents itself. We often see 'insurmountable obstacles' and 'absence of opportunities' all the time. The truth is even the biggest obstacle can easily be conquered if one wants to. When one door closes another one opens. But we concentrate on the closed door so much that we do not see the one that is open for us. Expect something good strongly and that expectation will energize your brain. Send suitable vibrations in all directions to materialize the same. If you are pessimistic, the brain follows your command and materializes nothing. Success and failure originate in your minds.

Position yourself to receive the result you are dreaming and working for, and they will appear as if from nowhere. If, on the other hand, you believe nothing good will ever come out of it, you will be accordingly frustrated. It all depends on whether you are ready to receive it or not or whether you are expecting the results or not. In an experiment with professional caterpillars (so named because they have the habit of following blindly each other), the researcher Fabre placed them in a circle. For twenty hours the caterpillars dutifully followed one another in a round. Later, he placed them around a saucer full of pine needles (they like it very much) and for 6 days they moved around and around and died of starvation.

An abundance of food was so close by. But they blindly followed their friends. Are you blindly following your internal maps and going after failures without actually beckoning the success that is a whisper away? Psychologists have correctly said that "when one is truly ready for a thing, it puts in its appearance." ☺☺

77. Who become your enemy?

The guy or woman whom you disliked at first sight is prone to become your enemy much more than those whom you liked at first sight. As the latter confirm to your standards and as their features harmonize with the features you love deeply, the chances are that they will remain in your friends or 'good people' list.

From the people we come across, we eventually make enemies of those whose appearance and features are incongruent with our mental map, and friends of those whose features and criteria are congruent with our maps.

The world is as we see it. People behave to us the way we see them. We tend to nourish a grudge and become harsher with those we dislike and they in turn show their resentment and dislike us. They understand our subconscious attitudes and reciprocate with equally inimical behaviours. We are thus creating our own enemies and friends under the influence of our mental maps.

Instead of complaining about the misbehaviours of others or trying to change them we should, I think, become aware of our mental maps and analyze how we see others. To our surprise we would find that most of those we hold 'bad' are not that bad after all. Pluck off the initial impressions from your mind and take them as good people and there will be nothing more to complain against them. We make our world.

Examine how you feel toward each person you meet, your neighbour, subordinate, colleague or superior. Impartially identify whether the first emotional impression (without any objective basis) influences your opinion of him/her. If the answer is yes you will have to restructure your map and make an assessment from an objective study of the person, his behaviour, efficiency, output, usefulness, honesty and integrity. Change you map before you can become a good friend, colleague, neighbour, manager, or supervisor. ☺☺

78. Ensure a good sleep

Just like eating sleep is a necessary factor for the survival of any species. Proper sleep is required to be healthy, to maintain one's brain sharp and creative. Sleep gives our body enough rest and prepares us for the tasks ahead during the next day. It is like offering your body and mind a mini-vacation. Lack of sleep induces stress and loss of concentration. It leads to numerous health problems like hyper tension and suppressed immune system. It is also a reason for decreased ability for decision making and math problem solving. Sleeplessness can make one eat more and thus augment weight-gain. Insomnia can lead to increased blood sugar level resulting in diabetes!

How many hours should one sleep? Some sleep 4 hours, others 8 and some on some days more than 10 hours! Opinions vary on the number of hours one should sleep. Very busy politicians sleep about 4-5 hours. There are those lazy guys who snore off for more than 12 hours too. Theories say enough sleep is important for compiling memories for transforming experiences and learning into improved performance. It could be safe to assume that in a 24-hour-cycle the human brain requires 8 hours of sleep. Sleeping 8 hours keeps your brain at the optimum efficiency; skin and body nourished and adds a few extra years to your life too.

There are mothers who spank the buttocks of their kids to wake up by half past five! These children must have had only about 6 hours sleep and they would doze off when they sit to read. The deficient sleep accumulates in the brain and whenever it gets an opportunity, the individual just dozes off. Adequate sleep is necessary for learning anything well. There are so many who struggle in the bed to get to sleep. There are as many advices too. One story goes like this: count from 1 to 100 or more (until you sleep). One lady started counting and she reached thousand without any sign of sleep descending on her. Nevertheless she continued and reached 10,000. Still sleep eluded her and she was still counting when it was dawn!

Some tips to ensure a good sleep:

1. Develop a bio-clock.
2. Sleep every day more or less at the same time so that your brain automatically prepares you to sleep by around that hour.
3. Do not engage in strenuous exercises a few hours before sleeping.
4. Shut your mind off from all disturbing thoughts as you lie down.
5. You can earmark a 'worry hour' for engaging in worry.

6. Do not read exciting stuff or engage in hot discussions before going to sleep.
7. If at all you want to read, do something hard, less exciting or boring.
8. Nothing should disturb you as you lie down, neither the sound of TV nor that of typing or conversations and loud shouts from the neighbours.
9. It is good to take some sweet or a little honey before going to bed.
10. Avoid strong tea or coffee.
11. Eat at least 3 hours before you go to bed that too a light dinner. The light should be subdued, and the bedding firm and comfortable.
12. When you lie down leave everything aside, free your mind to sleep.
13. Too much alcohol might send you to sleep immediately but the sleep will be short lived and not deep.
14. Engage in half an hour's physical exertion (brisk walking running or cycling with flexibility exercises) every day.
15. Follow a general bio-rhythm.

If you keep these points in mind you would be able to sleep peacefully for a duration your bio-clock is accustomed to and wake up fresh and recharged.

79. Prosperity begins with one's own thoughts

I had mentioned in another page 'you see what you believe'. Things happen when one believes. And thoughts and beliefs are absolutely one's own initiative. People's poverty can be removed only when they change their thoughts, when they become prosperity conscious. Every human being has the potential to create wealth and improve. They need only to change their perception. Nobody can create prosperity by subsidies or handouts.

Try to change the thought patterns of the poor and backward. They can easily create their own destiny – the way they want it. Success is their birthright too.

The earth gets infinite energy from the sun. Thus all of us have abundant energy resources. Even if 99.99% of all people are highly successful, there is still plenty of energy available for the remaining ones to succeed. Even if the whole oil-resources come to an end, there is still infinite energy left in the waters of the oceans, let alone the more tangible solar and tidal power potential available to mankind. Let those who want to make fortunes do so. There will be still infinite resources left for you. You can be so much more than what you are now. You have no control on what has happened to you. Accept it. But you have perfect control on your future.

Your time on this earth is meant for success, and happiness.

Start to create that destiny right from now.

80. Why do we fail?

Life is what you make it, good or bad, rich or poor, famous or mediocre, happy or unhappy. But in my experience, winning isn't about being rich, or having everything. It's about meeting your own goals, and living whichever way makes you happy. Why the majority do not succeed? They never know what they want. Without knowing what one wants how can one get it? They do not have specific, time bound goals. Too many goals will have the same effect as having none. Vagueness or general wishes is not going to help. "I want to go up," "I will make a lot of money," " I will win in life......" all these are vague and mostly meaningless statements.

People set a specific time bound goals or decide what they want precisely but they never start or take even the first step. Things seem too hard for them and they just remain in their comfort zone. If you are stuck at the first step itself, get moving. The only reason you haven't acted yet could be that you find it difficult to overcome the inertia, or you do not want to move out of your comfort zones. You could be afraid of failing or you may be thinking what others will think if you fail. No one has succeeded without failing. If you do not start there may not be any failure but you will never succeed too. Do not be afraid of what others will say; the only people who matter in your life are your dear ones and they already know you aren't perfect and that even if you fail they will accept you. The sad part is those who do not take that first step or retract after a few steps start believing they never can achieve it and forget about the whole thing.

People blame others for their failures. Stop blaming yourself or anyone else. If something negative happens or has already happened, life is still in your hands. Let us not forget this; let us not be overwhelmed by the stress of failure or set-backs. Do not forget you are not the only person in the world with problems. The pain of failure, loss and regret is something a lot of people feel daily. There are those who fail due to the lack of a realistic plan. They started in right earnest and went ahead but failed as there was no concrete, realistic plan to lead them to their goal. They give up after trying hard or when they face a difficult challenge or a temporary setback. Absence of review and corrective actions is will seal your fate. At the end of a particular period there should be evidences of advancement.

The absence of mentoring or a quality coach can be detrimental too. You have to acquire all the necessary skill and knowledge about your goals, update yourself of the latest developments and seek expert advice whenever required. There is no use in looking back and trying to correct yourself; you would have already reached a point of no-return. Failure is only a potential feedback. There is nothing called failure unless you mentally accept it. Everyone fails; those who succeed take it as a feedback, analyze the reasons and take corrective steps.

Hear what the great *Edison* speaks about failures, "Many of life's failures are people who did not realize how close they were to success when they gave up." "....When you are ready to quit you may be closer to the success you have been dreaming than you ever was."

81. All we know: we do not know

There is birth, growth, romance, tears, joy and death. Why do we take birth, grow, have passion for pleasure, money and possessions? Is not everything destined for darkness? Whence do I come from and whither do I go? Is there anything after the darkness? Is there anything before the light?

Are the birth into the light and the death into the darkness preplanned or accidental?

Who or what are we? Why do we, our planet and this Universe exist? All of us must have experienced these basic questions at some moment or other. Many have attempted to give answers to these questions, each from his/her particular perspective. The Theo-centric one's attribute everything here to a supernatural, omniscient, omnipotent and everlasting being. They find a purpose for creation. But who created God? Something cannot come from nothing or exist for all times. Examination on close quarters will rip this theory apart and reveal a chasm of darkness all around.

Science tries to explain everything in terms of physical, chemical, biological and gravitational laws. But they fail to explain the 'why' of it. *Emmanuel Kant* said,"Sepere Aude" or have the courage to know. He states that the content of the Universe, life and their destinies are still contentious or unresolved issues. There are a lot of scientists who believe that this Universe appeared out of nothing as quantum fluctuations of energy which grew into its present immensity. This was not inevitable but fortuitous. It could have not formed at all or formed in an altogether different way.

Similarly life, the arising of a self-organizing faculty whereby vitality with growth and reproduction kept alive, is itself a big mystery. Once the organic process got started, it became self-generating and self-changing. Man is the outcome of a series of events like evolution, mutations, and selection under climatic swings and cosmic impacts. There is no truth to maintain that evolution inevitably moves towards more exalted beings. Evolution can only explain the various forms of life. But why is all this happening? All that we know is we do not know.

82. Can you become Lincoln, Einstein, Picasso, Shakespeare?

"Anyone can reach anywhere." Thousands of books on the racks ('millions of copies of which are sold' every year) are there simply to state this. They talk about those who succeeded from the worst. Lincoln was poor, he could not attend school and he started working from 9; his entire life was one of failures. But he became the President of USA and one of the greatest men ever lived. They cite uneducated Edison who became a great inventor, Ford (illiterate) who became a great industrialist, Andrew Carnegie who rose up from poverty to riches, and the deaf, mute and blind Helen Keller who became a great lady. They even talk about a few Negroes who, against all odds, educated themselves and achieved success.

They say aloud, 'You are the captain of your soul; you are the master of your destiny.' But are we the makers of our destiny? Are we truly responsible for the heights or pits we find ourselves later in life? Do heredity, environment and experiences influence the way life unravels?

They have studied only those who tried and won. The vast majority of those who failed or continue to fail go unnoticed. They made rules (generalizations of success) from the lives of those who succeeded. But their study limits itself to the attempts they made, the setbacks and failures they had to face and the sweating they did. No attempt was made to ascertain the IQ, structure of the grey matter, their biology; childhood environment, parental interaction and experiences from infancy. Are these factors not influencing one's life? And without an in-depth of study of them are the generalizations valid?

Theoretically it may be possible to say any one can become great or rich irrespective of one's heredity and environment. There will be so many among you readers who feel that you had faced a number of adversities and came up irrespective of them. Millions of factors influence us from the moment of conception till we die. Some of the permutations and combinations are more positive than others. Without a deep analysis we cannot say whether we succeeded because of them or in spite of them.

Prince Charles is a great philanthropist and the future king of UK. He simply inherited billions and a throne was dangling over his head when he was born. Napoleon, Hitler, Lincoln, Nelson Mandela are all highly will-powered. How many living today can match that sort of a will? Mother Teresa, Martin Luther King, Gandhi, Father Damien, Florence Nightingale and Helen Keller lived to serve others. How many of us can be like them? Not even one in a million can become a great US president or other world leader. How many will have the tenacity and patience to go on experimenting until they invent something like the great scientists? How many among us have the physique and looks of Brad Pitt, John Travolta, Britney, Aiswarya or Madonna? There has been none with the IQ of Einstein or Charles Darwin ever since nor another Picasso, Michael Angelo or Leonardo da Vinci. As *Napoleon Hill* says, "If you cannot do great things by yourself, do small things in a great way."

83. You decide when 'to go'

Living to a healthy centenarian is not a dream any more. It is happening everywhere in the advanced nations. There are so many who have completed a century and going strong. Even in the underdeveloped ones, those who know and apply the secrets live beyond one hundred years. It is altogether another matter that man's average life will be above 100 years in a few decades from now. Man may eventually conquer ageing and death itself. There are scientists who believe that this may happen in our life time itself. There will come a time when man will die when he wants to.

Let us now concentrate on living beyond hundred without the usual old-age diseases and decrepitude or retaining youthfulness to the last. We want to keep the agility of our limbs, the power of our bran and memory and all sensory capabilities intact throughout our lives. Most of us today think that we have to grow old soon and that we will become senile with impaired hearing, arthritis, weak brittle and thin bones, high BP, high cholesterol sagging skin, less eyesight, less strength and poor hearing.

People think they will become abandoned, disowned, useless and unwanted. Is it not our expectation that produce the result? After all, expectations are self-fulfilling. Suppose you strongly desire to retain youthfulness, delay ageing and live longer, that will become the reality. Haven't you heard an elderly parent declaring 'I may not be around for the next Christmas.' In all probability he may not be here. Your brain is a computer. It functions as per a written program. If you continuously think that you will die before the next Christmas, in all probability the brain will carry out that command. On the other hand, if you continuously think about your goals to be achieved after your eighties and nineties and the wonderful life you are going to have, it is certain that your super computer will accomplish the dreams in a similar vein. But without desiring long life you will not get one. Everything starts with an intense dream. That is not enough, of course. You need something to live for at any moment of time. There are to be worthy goals after which you set your gaze and you need to be purposefully engaged all the time. This is perhaps the next mantra to keep you in eternal youth.

84. Giving: the great secret of success

Life has taught me a great lesson: the beauty in giving. The greatest souls that have grazed this planet are those who gave themselves up for others fully and unconditionally. Let it be *Mother Teresa, Father Damien, Gandhi, Martin Luther King Jr.* or *Abraham Lincoln*......they surpassed all living souls with their selfless service to the needy.

As *Winston Churchill* once said, "We make a living by what we get; we make a life by what we give."

Our lives will be very much less fruitful if we are not giving what we have to others. It can be motivation, knowledge riches, time, comforting words; it can be anything that alleviates others' pain or something that make others' life richer and more meaningful. It is this realization that motivates the rich philanthropists to give significant portions of their wealth to the poor.

I have noted that all great leaders and thinkers of history have opted for selfless lives. I also remember very often the ancient Chinese saying, 'a little fragrance always clings to the hand that gives roses.' Those who have the attitude, 'May I serve you,' enjoy life far better than those who are constantly after material possessions, power or professional advancement.

Giving can be its own reward. But there is another aspect that a lot of us have failed to recognize. Giving is a form of energy that not only helps the recipient but it bounces back in a greater measure to the giver. The backward journey of this energy is often shrouded in mystery that the giver is not aware of it instantly nor is it immediately perceptible to the world at large. The giver receives more than what he gave out if he did so without any personal motivation whatsoever.

'The hand that gives is the hand that gathers.' Ancient and modern philosophers maintain that the secret to wealth is giving. When you spend money it goes out and touches so many and depending on your mental attitude it may bring back abundance.

No wonder a famous Arab author, *Al Koran* advises people to bless the bills before you part with them so that it blesses all those they touch. He wants us to command the money to go out, feed the hungry, clothe naked and come back a million fold.

During my seminars I often ask the participants, 'will you get something if you work more than what you are paid for?' At other times I ask them: 'if you go the extra mile in your work, who is going to be benefitted?'

Most of them would answer thus: 'the employer will get the benefit.'

'Won't you be benefitted in any way?'

After quite a bit of reflection someone would say, 'we will develop too and our self-esteem will go up.'

Well, you will be much more benefitted than the owner. You will be rewarded hundredfold by the Universe who is a just an employer. When you give out selflessly, the great universal Watchdog is going to reward you. It is certain that you will add tons of self-esteem and you will increase your confidence levels. Further, you have invested in yourself and you have already become more valuable at the market place. When you go out for an interview the added self respect and esteem will make you ask for more pay as you know you are willing to give more than he is going to pay back to you.

The Bible mentions that whenever anyone feeds or clothes a destitute he does so to God himself. Well I think there is no good in the world which can come anywhere near the act of giving, selfless giving in particular.

When I train youngsters the art of developing self-confidence, I always emphasize selfless giving as the shortcut to the development of this crucial quality. In fact I tell them to check before they sleep every day whether they did some help to someone without expecting anything in return.

It can be helping a blind person to cross the road.

It can be feeding a beggar who is hungry.

It can be offering a soothing smile to a stranger who is in tension.

It can be offering a dollar bill to someone who is dire need and whom you do not know.

It can be removing a stone from a foot path so that others are not hurt.

It can be picking up plastic bags and bottles from around a public place to make it tidier.

It can be pardoning a motorist who has splashed mud on your dress as he sped by.

It can be a great act of giving if:

You keep a radiant smile as you crisscross the pathways of life.

You spare some time to take an injured stranger to a hospital.

You give out a certain portion of your wealth to an unknown poor man or woman.

You help your employer earn through your extra work, vigilance and care.

You spend some time with the old to brighten their day.

You give your seat for an invalid in a crowded bus.

Let me share a great secret to become richer. start giving a portion of what you earn or what you posses. What goes out comes back. Selfless giving ensures manifold return. All the rich people of this planet are inclined to help others. And that could be one of the reasons why they become richer. They get back what was given out, in true charity, hundredfold. Giving is a sure way to receive more.

Blessed are those who can give without remembering. That could be why our present world is getting filled with those who want to give without any string attached. They are quick to part with a part of what they have earned as they know giving has a superior value when one does so quickly and not waiting for to be asked,

The best way you can evaluate a person is by how much he gives and by how much he feels for others in his wallet. Giving is always a thermometer of one's love towards others. When it comes to giving some people stop at nothing. 'Give all you can,' is an excellent formula for a successful life.

Living for others is the best way to live. That could be why *Henry Drummond* once said, 'there is true happiness only in giving.' Before we conclude let me remind you *Arthur Schweitzer's* words, "There is no higher religion than human service. To work for the common good is the greatest creed."

85. Has your life been hard so far?

Have you toiled hard and reached nowhere? If you stick your finger in the fire, it gets burnt. This is really easy as the effect comes immediately after the cause. But it is not easy to figure out what has caused your present.

At the end of a winding, long, dark tunnel there is always light and plenty of it. If the tunnel is long and difficult the whole world would be aligned to receive you as a hero when you emerge. You can never get such an acclaim if the going has been rather easy. You can see light ahead of the darkness now surrounding you, and walk confidently forward. You can also curse it and accept defeat. The freedom is yours.

There is no defeat however hard the situation may be. I was reading about Oscar Pistorius the other day, a double amputee who is the fastest man on 'no legs' He is the world record holder in the 100, 200, and 400 meters events (sport Class T44). He was born on November 22, 1986 and is a South African sprint runner. A man running on artificial legs can be faster than all of us! Stephen Hawkins cannot even lift a finger, talk, walk, stand, sit or eat. He is all paralyzed with Neuron Motor Deficiency. Only his brain is intact. But he is the greatest scientist living. He is occupying Newton's Chair in Oxford University! He has turned into flood light the darkness that surrounds his life.

86. Don't lie down licking your wounds

French philosopher *Rousseau* said all are born free and equal. Positive thinkers stress that we make what we are, that we are totally free to grow and develop. Many kids are born into abject poverty, with low IQ and they are unloved and unwanted. Many are born blind, crippled, deaf, mute and feeble minded or with the propensities for sicknesses and mental disorders including madness. A child born in a nation like USA, UK, Germany Norway, Sweden or Australia have better opportunities to develop and grow than one from Somalia, Ethiopia , Bangladesh or India. The latter may not even survive childhood. They will not go to school and will be malnourished and sick. One's biology, the structure of the grey matter (both inherited) and early childhood experiences do affect one's responses and behaviour. Success very much depends on one's IQ and EQ for both of which the individual is not responsible.

If parents do not love you or if they fight all the time leaving you to fend for yourself, you will not develop like another who is loved, accepted and given proper care. The home environment has a say in determining how you grow, keep your relationships, interact with the others and meet life's challenges.

How many have the persistence like Edison, Colonel Sanders, Henri Ford or the will of Nelson Mandela, Napoleon, Hitler, Gandhi or Martin Luther King?

How many can overcome failures like Abraham Lincoln? How many of us can challenge adversities like Helen Keller?

How many will dare like Mark Ingles (a double amputee who scaled Mount Everest)?

How many of us have the IQ of Albert Einstein?

How many can sing like Jim Reeves or Michael Jackson?

How many can paint like Picasso or Michael Angelo?

How many has the bodily adornments of Elizabeth Taylor, or Brad Pitt?

How many can write like Shakespeare?

The great ones seem to be more born than made.

But we need not be envious of those who are lucky (they did not ask for it). The world is not bothered whether you were born poor or rich, with high or low IQ and EQ, in a home of love or strife. It wants you to win; it goes with the winners only. No arguments please. No questions entertained. That is how the game of life is played.

Who wants to know your history? The only relevant question is: 'have you succeeded?'

The world does not want to know where you plan to reach.

What are you now? That is all what counts. If you don't want to come up that is your problem. There might be some negatives in your person ingrained or inherited from your parents and early childhood, but you have enough to succeed-a normal brain. And by intense desire, sheer work and persistence you can reach where you want to. You may not be able to become like the truly great ones. And you need not. But succeed you must and you can. Don't lie down licking your wounds.

87. IQ may not be enough at the workplace

Having a brilliant academic background is great but it may not be helpful if one plans to work in the real world with real people with all their foibles and faults. You need the ability to work in a team to succeed. If a brilliant guy has poor social relations skills and cannot cope with stress, he fails.

They are highly qualified but not competent. They may mechanically execute a task but lack that something needed to work in a team. Or, they may be technically sound but are not able to neither control their emotions nor understand their team members properly.

Their work output may be superlative too. But they are not easy to get along with and they keep upsetting others. They may fail to solve problems and understand others' thinking patterns. They may not easily adapt to situations nor change behaviour as and when required. They may not be optimistic in the face of adversity.

This is a classic case of IQ vs. EQ. With the challenges of today, I feel being a good EI person will only take you further.

Is the Academic world designed almost everywhere to remove imagination and creativity from the students? Why aren't they exposed to different social settings and taught ways to cope with stress?

Communication and attitude affect the performance of high IQ people in the corporate world. They are poor communicators and they have a poor attitude, often arrogant. In the corporate world, we need to work as a team and communicate effectively our views and hear alternative views; we need to be open. Bookish knowledge is not practical knowledge.

When we are dealing with people let us remember we are not dealing with creatures of logic. We are dealing with creatures of emotion. The universities do not equip students to tackle emotions. Brilliance measured by tests alone may not succeed in the workplace.

88. Lessen worry; Become merry

A newlywed girl started weeping profusely without waking up from bed in the morning. Her mother asked why she was crying. "May be someday my husband would be going in a ship he told me yesterday he loves sea-travel and it may meet with an accident and drown and he will die."

Well, this may look unreasonable. She is weeping over an imagined situation which may never come to pass. But we all do this sort of things very often: we blow up something that may never come to pass and worry. And we know worry will strangle or choke us off.

Many of us feel we do something only when we worry. A day of worrying is exhausting, harder than work. It leads nowhere; analyzing an imagined event threadbare makes your body and mind simply paralyzed.

People waste their lives stuck in a state of constant worry. They worry about their children's poor grades, future, work, about the attitude of the boss, relationships with others, diseases, enemies, travel, the leak that has been developed in the roof.

Worrying is a help if it makes you to take action, to solve a problem, avoid bad things or prepare you for the worst. But that rarely happens and mostly worry becomes a problem of its own. Some of us even worry about worrying too. Worry induces fears and sends one's anxiety levels soaring which interfere with one's day-today life. It is normally a habit and this can be overcome by training your brain to look at life from a better perspective. The greatest comforting thought is that almost everyone worries—great leaders, painters, singers, authors, and rich, poor, all.

I have heard about an old lady who worried all day long. But her real worry starts by the sunset. She worries just about anything and everything and the funniest thing is that none of her worries has ever materialized. Studies done on worry show that more than 95 percent of them never happen. And the remaining will happen whether you worry or not. So why worry at all?

Worry really burns us off while we are alive just like a pyre burns off a dead body. Worry does not help tomorrow's problems in any way and the sad part is that it takes away today's happiness. When we worry about the future, we are destroying the future itself. Worrying does not help anyone; still, many find it hard to stop it.

Worry comes uninvited and most of us feel it is not within our control to get away from this nagging problem. They rob you of the ability to laugh, love and share joy with your dear ones.

Is there no way to control the same or at least mitigate its debilitating effects? Constant worrying takes a heavy toll as it gives sleepless nights and makes your days edgy and confused. You may even believe that constant worrying will lead to diseases or that it may drive you crazy.

Well, if you sit and worry when it takes possession of your mind, it will bother you more and smother your faculties. Worrying rarely leads to solutions. You're no more prepared to deal with them should they actually happen no matter how much time you spend brooding over even the worst case scenarios.

Distraction could be a way of escape; do something that can absorb you fully like engaging in your hobby, playing with your children, enjoying a warm bath, watching a hilarious movie, talking to someone you love, taking a walk in a quiet beautiful place, hearing a song you love, reading a book you cherished all along or playing your favourite game. But this is no permanent solution it will only lessen the tension worry induces.

But remember that telling yourself to stop worrying does not help in the long run. Your suppression of anxious thoughts makes them stronger and more persistent over a longer period.

Why not assign a period for worrying every day? Half an hour you sit for 'worrying'. Follow the same place and time for worry: earmark say, 5:30pm in the bedroom. During this 'worry period', you can worry about anything and everything but the rest of the day must be free of it. If worry thoughts prop up in between, assign it for the worry time when you can indulge in it to your heart's content. Making a worry list for the worry time is found to be helpful too. Postponing worry helps as it breaks the habit of dwelling on any worry that props up then and there. Slowly you get more control on the worrying habit.

Even deep, slow breathing and exhaling will calm you down and reduce the intensity of worry. While relaxed thus, focus on what you can do to solve the problem rather than what you cannot do.

There is a very practical way to get rid of the tension from worry: relax your muscles. Take each limb of your body and hold it tight while you count up to 5. Release the tension and move it slowly sideways saying to yourself, relax, relax, relax. Start with your legs, then the buttocks, backside, neck, forehead, eyes, mouth, chest, stomach and hands. If you have relaxed each muscle in your body, the tension induced by the worry would have melted away.

Have you heard the old saying, 'an optimist laughs to forget and the pessimist forgets to laugh?' It is very much true. The only paradox is: there are more pessimists. We are all holding our facial muscles taut and we do not let them ease out for a moment nor relax them in a smile that will guarantee a better appearance. Smiling is an anti-dot for worry too. Worry cannot reside in a person who keeps a smile. A good laugh is the medicine. If you frown, you worry more.

Make sure you are not caught up in a worry cycle. We worry about something now. When it eases off but another worry crops up and when this one fades away a third is waiting to enter.

Thinking about all the things that could go wrong does not make life any more predictable or keep off bad things from happening. It is not possible to be certain about everything in the future. What is the need to be certain about? Let there be some uncertainty. Why should we predict bad things when the possibility for a bad occurrence is very every low?

89. A new year resolution

2013 has arrived. An old year has been rung out and a new one rung in. The New Year gives us all a lot of hope. We can forget all our mistakes and shortcomings. We can dream and restart in right earnest.

The past is past; let us bury the past. Here is the freshness of yet another year. One where we can keep our resolutions and promises we have made to ourselves.

Have you made New Year resolutions? Like we did last year and the year before? Let them not become nasty reminders of the broken promises we made to ourselves. Let us not make any for the sake of making them. Let us make them only if we intend to carry them out, come what may.

Let us resolve to go a little more to love our dear ones, spend more time with our kids, love more our partner, forgive their shortcomings, ignore their bad habits, sacrifice our egos a little more, go that extra mile to make him/her happy. Let us learn to give more and help more. After all, life's pleasures lie in loving and giving. Let us resolve to invest in ourselves: learn a new skill, acquire more ideas on what we do or get a fresh diploma; start dreaming for a better job with a higher pay. Let us resolve to bring down our fab by 10lbs or whatever, start exercising every day and make ourselves fitter in mind and body.

We have just 365 days before another year comes whistling by. Each day, each hour and each minute is important. We have the same time Mother Teresa, Michelangelo, Helen Keller or Leonardo Da Vinci had. The quality of our life is decided by how we spend each minute. Let each minute be fruitful and happy. Let us resolve not to waste a single minute of a single day. Let us make this year of the 80-100 odd years we have on this planet a memorable one which we will truly live.

90. Say a big thank you

Today, you live in peace. Think about war times when lives were lost so easily, and when pain, suffering, and poverty were everywhere. Now you have your loved ones near you. Many had lost them in war, in natural calamities and in accidents. Today, you live in an age of medical breakthroughs and communication revolution. You can talk to your dear ones abroad over the Skype instantly. In the past, remember, letters took months to arrive, if at all they did. Now you send an email and it is delivered in seconds. Even kings in the past didn't have a fraction of the entertainment options you have today like the television, movie, electronic games, travels, adventure tourism, just to name a few.

Now you can update your knowledge in any subject as every knowledge is there in the net at home. Years before, you had to search it in an appropriate book in a library and a few centuries before, knowledge was transmitted orally; writing had not been invented yet.

You are blessed with friends, relatives, lover, partner, father, mother, grandparents, teachers, pets, house, garden, TV, computers, automobiles, aircrafts, ships, trains, fridge, job, health, food, entertainments, moon, stars, rainbow, sunset, sunrise, rain, snow, nature, animals, music, dance, nightclubs, strangers and lots of love. There is really a lot to be thankful for. We are not aware of these and we take them for granted. Sometimes we need to experience a loss to appreciate the value of what we have. Become grateful for all you have this moment, this day. A thankful heart is very important to our happiness. Enjoy the beauty, richness, love and opportunities that exist in life. Appreciate those who help us or give nice things to us.

Let us reframe painful or disappointing events as opportunities for doing something good. Let people who love you know that you are grateful to them. Be thankful for what you have, as you never know when it will be gone.

As an anonymous poet has sung:

If your arteries have hardened and arthritis have slowed your gait,

Or if your dancing days are over, or if any other condition afflicts you,

think of others with more pain like the fellow in the wheel chair or the one without hands or legs,

and be grateful for the use of the right arm that can write a letter,

for the eyes that can savor every flower, bird and tree,

for the ears that can tune in the sounds they make and above all your brain, the greatest asset. There are many who are mad, retarded or imbeciles who cannot use this wonderful faculty.

You cannot welcome more abundance into your life until you have said to the Universe truly, "Hey, thanks for all I have". Place yourself in a better mood by being thankful. You will find you are in a much more optimistic state after you have spent a few minutes reflecting about your blessings and feeling grateful for them. Compassion and kindness will probably fill your heart.

Helen Keller was blind, deaf and mute; still she thought she was blessed and tried to cheer those who were blind. Mark Ingles, whose legs were amputated below the knee in 1982, as they were frost-bitten while stuck in a snow cave for 13 days during mountaineering, feels there is a lot left to be thankful about. He is grateful he is alive and he conquered Mount Cook in 2002 and Mount Everest in 2006. And these days he is travelling around inspiring others to enjoy and appreciate this life. If a person without both eyes, ears, vocal chords or both legs has so much to be happy about we sure can be happier and say a bigger thank you to this dear life and the Universe which gave birth to us.

91. You can be lucky too

Generally, people do not know how much they can accomplish. They think that only a few are destined for success and all the others are just unlucky or destined to be mediocre. 'There is a grey cloud over my head,' they say. Or 'I have been set like this.' They feel they have effectively no control over their lives. They go wherever the river of life takes them.

There is no luck or ill luck. Luck comes when your thoughts and actions are streamlined to what you want. Ill luck comes when you idle away your time, do your work perfunctorily and accept whatever life does out to you. The truth about luck is contained in the following verse of a famous poet:

"He worked by day and toiled by night;
He gave up play and some delight;
Dry books he read, new things to learn.
And forged ahead success to earn;
He plodded on with faith and pluck,
And when he won men called it luck."

The world fails to see the efforts and toil one does before he triumphs. No one is doomed to failure. It comes because of intense desire, full-time focus and controlled thoughts. There has been a conventional belief that you have to earn success either by doing hard work or by doing always good. This is no longer true. It is all vibrations. When you think and believe something with all your heart, all your soul and all your body you will get it. When you see your goals as already achieved in your thoughts, feelings and emotions it will become a reality very soon.

92. Your brain is like a god!

You have a belief that god (whatever it means to you) will grant you everything you wish. He loves you and makes you do what is good for you. Well, we do not know god; there are so many contradictory versions. However, we have a faulty which is an all powerful god.

Brain is timeless: it was formed in a miniscule way as life germinated on this planet from the combination of abundant substances in the energy supplied by the sun. Through evolution, it grew in volume and weight and became more and more complicated (present average weight is 1.3-1.5kg and volume 1130ccs to 1260cc. The weight of human brain is 2% of its body's weight and that of a sperm whale is just .06% (human brain is 33 times bigger). Intelligence increased with the increase in volume and weight.

Brain's functioning is a miracle in itself. *Robert Berge* estimates that the capacity of the brain is around 3 terabytes (anything between 1-10 terabytes). The human brain contains between 50-100 billion neurons and each of which interfaces with 1,000 to 100,000 other neurons through 100 trillion synaptic junctions. The total information storage capacity of the synapses in the cortex would be of the order of 500 to 1,000 terabytes. The nearest mammal, the baboon has only about 14 billion neurons.

Why do we have such an amazing machine within us? It is certainly not to carry on the bodily functions. Even one hundredth of it is not required to do that. It stores miraculous powers. If you are thousands of miles away from home and if something happens seriously to you, your mother at home will get inkling almost immediately. Brain has telepathic powers. It was reported that *Yuri Geller* could bend metal objects by concentrating on them and even the spoons and forks in the kitchen cabinets of those who watched the program got bent too! While you travel in a bus, if you concentrate on the person sitting in front of you he will turn back in a few minutes. Your brain has special powers. There are people who can read a book opened behind a curtain without seeing it. This is called clairvoyance. If you give repeated suggestions in a relaxed state, to cure an affliction you suffer from, it is almost certain your subconscious mind will do the healing. If you dream a goal with belief or intensity at least half the time you are awake for a year or two it is certain you will get it. But if the thoughts are highly emotionalized like when you want to marry your loved one, the materialization happens very fast, regardless of the hurdles on the way.

Brain brings about very 'miracle' that happen in every religious place in the world. The 'holy' places make you believe your prayers will be answered and eventually you do get some answers. These are the handiwork of your brain as anything one believes fully is eventually materialized by one's brain. The howls, shouts, singing and flashing lights of churches and temples or a mysterious silence prevailing there help to make your beliefs intense and emotionalized speeding up the eventual materialization. There is nothing the human brain cannot accomplish. It can cure you of any disease; it can bring you riches, fame, prosperity or anything else.

93. Problem is with you, not with the world

There is nothing in the brain when a child is born into the world. There is no knowledge, no prejudice, and no inclination. It is like an untilled land. One can direct or make use of it anyway one wants to. But through his five senses, information flows in uninterrupted and he soon forms a world view. He creates a map through which he views this world and its people. If the map has been well-formed, he would see the world right; a distorted map would find problems with all. How one has been programmed to view this life and the people around will determine one's entire life.

Any event will be seen through the colour of your map. A person with a good map would look for lessons in a failure and start scheming for another attempt. When faced with a problem, a bad map would see the whole world crumbling with darkness all around with no ray of hope.

An ill formed person finds bad things. All people around and those he comes across are bad too. A well-formed one sees many good everywhere. Instead of trying to correct the world, correct your map, correct your personality.

If you want to like others, you have to first like yourself. If you have to appreciate others, you have to have self-esteem. If you hate yourself or have a lot of diffidence, in all profanity, you will be a faultfinder and a problem creator. The problem is with you and not with the world. Change yourself and the world will be automatically changed.

One need not cry over one's bad childhood, bad parents, bad neighbours, poverty, lack of education and the not-so-good-looks; one can succeed by changing one's map and by controlling one's thoughts. If one does not make use of his brain and change his map, he will be a failure regardless of the attributes he has. If one does not love himself, the whole world will look bad. One has to try to be a success to tart loving oneself and feel good. ☺☺

94. Differentiate between right and wrong

The world we live in, David Hume tells us, is "the first rude essay of some infant deity who afterwards abandoned it, ashamed of his lame performance"; or the work "of some . . . inferior deity, the object of derision to his superiors"; or, perhaps, "the production of old age and dotage in some superannuated deity." In any case, Hume says, it is scarcely what we would have expected "from a very powerful, wise, and benevolent Deity." Or, as Woody Allen sums it up, considering God's advantages, He must be regarded as an underachiever.

The story is that, at a deeper level beyond what we can see around us, the universe is governed, fundamentally, by an all-powerful force that will, someday, make everything all right. The force may go under the name of Jehovah, Allah, or dialectical materialism, or it may be that principle of goodness in the universe that assured Gandhi that satyagraha would triumph – but we are always promised an inevitable victory. Not one of these movements has ever had the guts to say to its adherents what every honest general must admit to his officers – "Jeez, I have no idea how this will turn out, but we're fighting on the right side, so let's go do our best."

There are two fundamental problems with making up these stories about guaranteed victory. First, forcing yourself to believe in factual claims for which there is no evidence turns your brain to mush, equipping you only for further acts of self-deception. Practice this habit of mental self-abuse long enough, and you will be left in the desperately enfeebled mental condition of the President of the United States, unable to perform the most modest act of factual analysis. Second, the purpose of these narratives is to make the universe look better, not to make people act better.

What if we chose, instead, to begin in exactly the opposite way? Instead of making up a myth to provide window-dressing for the universe, let us make up a myth to provide ourselves with moral backbone. As long as we are careful to bear in mind that it is a myth, the overall effect should be positive.

As you have no doubt guessed by now, I have such a myth to propose. Let us suppose that the theory of reincarnation is correct – that, after each lifetime is over, each soul wakes up in a new human body, beginning life over again as a baby. Now, nothing, of course, is beyond the power of God, so let us make one further assumption: that the soul may be reincarnated centuries after the death of the previous body, or – listen carefully, now – centuries before the death of the last owner. I could die today and be reincarnated, say, as the infant Lincoln. Or the infant Booth. Granting these two assumptions, reincarnation and reincarnation that occurs backwards in time, we are now ready to present the myth in its final and complete form: THERE IS, IN FACT, ONLY ONE HUMAN SOUL. IT HAS BEEN AND WILL BE REINCARNATED BILLIONS OF TIMES. For as long as there have been or will be people, they have all shared and will share only this one soul.

It may be helpful to call to mind the process of sewing – how the thread passes down through layers of material and then back up through layers of material, again and again and again. So this one human soul passes forward through life and then back in time for a fresh start, over and over again.

95. Celebrate life

In any failure-however deep and painful-there are hidden elements of success and brilliant rays to guide and lead us up to light. Behind any deed, there is a good intention. There are streaks of goodness in everything. Anyone can be happy at any moment.

Our enemies are those whom we see as enemies. If we hate someone, he will hate us back. If we love someone, he will love us back too.

This world is full of good things. Those balancing rocks, gurgling rivulets, greeneries, fragrant blooms, tranquil lakes, and the whole beauty of this nature has been specially arranged for you. Things happen here so very naturally and in perfect harmony. See how the moon rounds the earth, the earth and the moon round the sun, which along with all its planets and satellites rounds the galactic nucleus in absolute precision and harmony. A small seed germinates with tender shoots and grow into a big and beautiful tree. All these have been going on here so very naturally for billions of years! This natural harmony can be witnessed in the birth of a child, the blooming of a bud and the downward meandering flow of a stream.

Let us celebrate this life. We are so very lucky to have taken birth in this Universe during this advanced epoch. We are emanating from and going into this Universe. Little bundles of energy gave birth to us and they will return to the universal storehouse to live forever. We have no death; we will always live. Let us celebrate each second of the minor we have been allotted down here as humans.

Let us be grateful to our parents who gave birth to us, to the teachers who led us to the world of knowledge, to all our relatives, neighbours and friends who have loved and made us happy. We have taken birth to enjoy every second. There is joy in every cell of a new born baby. Let us love all, be grateful to everything in this world and make our life a thing of joy.

96. Amuse yourself when in a snarl

There is a terrific traffic jam. You can move neither forward nor backward. You are trapped and it is terrible. You will be late for your office and your boss will pounce upon you. You will lose the business deal you have so painstakingly worked upon. You may be late for the important meeting the participants of which had been so painstakingly brought together. You may miss the flight or you may be late for the lecture you had wanted to attend so badly. Your partner would be terribly angry; after all, you had promised to be there in another twenty minutes and now you don't know when you will reach. Even if you tell the truth, she might not believe as you had already given excuses of a big snarl for being late before when you were not stuck in a traffic jam.

Thinking about all this, you become angry, tense, and you do not know what to do. You look out trying to know whether any soul knows what has happened. You keep looking at your watch with a furrowed forehead and grim face. You are at your worst. You can feel every cell of your body becoming taut and the way you suppress your anger, despair and helplessness. It is indeed an ordeal and time seems to stand still.

Anyway, you are hooked. By becoming tense and nervous, the situation is not going to improve at all. You have to wait anyway until the bloody thing ends.

Sit there behind the wheel and try to look into the sky. Observe the clouds that float like white cotton puffs, see the designs they make as they move, and try to figure out a meaning for the patterns. Bring the window glasses down (if it is not freezing outside) and feel the gentle breeze whispering by. Hear the chirpings of birds. Does the wind waft up to you a fragrance? Can you see some treetops swaying in the breeze?

Bring a favourite spot to your mind and recall all its details. See the colourful plants and hedges, gurgling rivulets, panoramic views of the valleys, get the scents and hear every sound. If you have the family album in the car, see you child or partner and just keep looking at them. You will be instantly relieved. May be you can read a book you keep in the car or play your favourite song in the car stereo. It will instantly lift and relax you. Sing or hum a tune you love. As you enjoy the music, give your hand and face a massage.

Look around, you will find a lot to amuse yourself. Observe how the other passengers react to the jam. You can of course use this time to do your business calls. Call your office and leave all the necessary instructions for the day.

Or, call your dear friend, your child or the one you love and simply talk to him/her.

See, how you have become a stress-busting superhero. As we lead a much-stressed life most of the time, you may not be aware that you are in tension during a snarl. Become aware and resort to one of the above and when the jam is over drive on and arrive there fresh with all your mental energies intact. If you stay there with the built up stress for an hour or so you will be a spent horse and you will be underperforming all day.

97. Sure recipe for perfect health

Every cell of a new born baby is pure like a dew drop. The blood vessels are transparent like a clear glass. How does it then become sick later? Eating fatty junk food is one and not exercising is another reason. Children are not trained to eat fruits, peas, lentils, vegetables and nuts. Instead, they get ice creams, cold drinks and fast foods. All these with alcohol, drugs and smoking bring in a host of health problems.

Almost 90 percent of all diseases are due to the lifestyle of man. If one takes more food, fat gets deposited on the walls of blood vessels or elsewhere. Overweight, non-exercise and the intake of salt coupled with the genetic propensity leads to BP, diabetes, cholesterol and heart diseases. Excess food-even carbohydrates-are deposited as fat in the body. If you are overweight your heart has to pump more blood, lungs has to provide more oxygen to more cells; stomach, liver, pancreas intestines, blood vessels and all have to work more exhausting vital organs and the entire system.

If a disorder sets in, every living thing has a natural ability to get well. If a bone is broken, it will be joined if the broken pieces are kept together to heal. Doctors simply keep the broken bones in position and plaster to ensure they do not get disturbed during the healing process. If a blood vessel is cut, blood clots to prevent blood loss and the spot get okay without any outside help. If the cut is large, the clotting may not work and hence the wound need to be cured for the body to do the healing.

If an animal is sick, he does not eat (but drinks water) and rests completely until he is cured. If humans get sick, we do not stop eating, we do not take complete rest for natural healing to be effective and complete. The disease worsens and we approach a hospital or resort to medicine to be cured.

Generally eat less, that too whole grain, vegetables including leafy ones and deep coloured fruits. Take less sugar and salt; avoid fast food and fired stuff, take at least 8-10 glasses of water daily. Do aerobic, muscle building and flexibility exercises and meditate for 15 minutes. Keep your memory and brain in excersing mode. Be purposefully engaged and, become grateful to the Universe for this life and love your dear ones. This is a sure recipe for perfect health.

98. Let's not oppress women

Women in the Indian states like Kerala are subjected to pinching, stalking, hooting, and singing with sexual undertones and flashing of objects. I still remember a person who used to piss openly standing towards his neighbour's house when he knew the lady of the house is outside doing her daily chores. He used to go on passing until the lady, noticing him holding his manhood in the guise of urinating, had to go inside expressing her displeasure.

No girl-whatever be her age-can pass alone through the roads during full day light without inviting derisive comments. Imagine her plight at night or after dusk has fallen. A bevy of loitering youth or middle-aged people will start stalking her as if every woman is available for sex. Even foreign tourists are not spared these days. This made an Italian traveler comment: 'Kerala is the most sex-hungry place in the world!'

Women here experience eve teasing in every phase of their life every day, every where: at school, at college, at the work-place, in the public transport vehicles, in the parks, cinema halls, festival sites... It is a clear case of sexual harassment but most women prefer to ignore it. They are advised to dress 'modestly' when they go out and come home early.

Men are free to dress the way they want to; they can flaunt their chest or buttock muscles (remember today's low waste stuff) or walk half-naked in the house or even outside. They dress to their convenience and comfort. Nobody can question it, let alone women. But women have to conform to society (men) approved norms; even if it is scorching hot and humid. Are they not equal human beings too? Are they simply sex objects of men?

Even if they are cover up fully from head to foot, there is a lot of sexual harassment. As they try to board a bus or train they are subjected to a squeeze here, a touch there or a poking in the most undesirable places. There are those who make it a point to press against a woman in a crowded bus or train and enjoy the pleasure of continuing with the pressure maintained at peak levels. If she does not protest, the thing will go on until the natural pressure releasing system comes to work.

There is the story of a man who followed a woman traveling in a bus for 15 kilometers. When she alighted and shouted at him he said casually: "I have not touched you yet and all that I want is to ask you out for tea." What a way to ask a strange girl for a date!

This happens in a country where people claim to be very cultured. Well, women have been discriminated against throughout history in all lands; but this attitude has changed and now men and women are equal and they march together respecting each other. It is a pity there are nations a century or two behind.

Men and boys are free to go out, drink in a pub or hang out to their heart's content but girls have restrictions in everything everywhere. Last year a bevy of youth beat up women who were drinking bear in a Mangalore pub. Let women have fun and let them enjoy life as men do.

Today every girl past 10 feels insecure to go out alone; she feels her body can be trounced or molested and lurking men all around can defile the virtues she holds dear. Is this culture?

99. Live your lives!

As I sit in front of my laptop to begin, the words of *Theodore Roosevelt* come to my mind: "Far better is to dare mighty things, to win glorious triumphs, even though checkered by failure ....than rank with those poor spirits who neither enjoy much nor suffer much, because they live in a gray twilight that knows no victory and no defeat." Well, how many of us are cut out for great victories and triumphs which this great man is talking about? Not many. And none of you will enjoy great victories if your mind does not want it.

None of us is destined to wallow in misery or suffer throughout our life. None of us need to just 'to pull on' doing whatever little needed to be paid, feed our family, pay the bills and merge into the darkness ahead.

We adjust with a job we do not like, with a partner we do not love, and spend our days knowing very well that we are not living our life. This is going to be our greatest sorrow. We have failed in our mission here. We have not truly lived a single day on this planet. It is true that we got this life unasked. We have been lucky enough to be born in this century, in this country amidst abundance and advancement in every sphere of human activity. We are lucky that diseases did not cut short our life during early infancy or in childhood. We have been able to attend school, college and perhaps university to enrich ourselves. We have every comfort that our ancestors could not even dream of. But still in the heart of our hearts we are unhappy. We are not living our lives.

Our thoughts and beliefs have been confined by our prejudices; we have never risen above the limits that were set in our mental and material horizons. We have been stuck with the precepts and tenets of our religion; we have been fettered by our cultural traditions. We have been leading a small life all the way convinced we are only capable that much and not more. Break these limiting beliefs! Live the life you enjoy, you are destined for. Do the job you love, spend the free time the best way you want. Love those whom you like and say good-bye feeling fulfilled and happy.

100. Can I succeed?

Answer the following questions and see the rating at last to know your chances.

1. Have you taken up a profession you innately love?

   ☐ Yes ☐ No

2. How do you spend your free time?

   ☐ Watching TV ☐ Chatting with friends ☐ Idling away the time ☐ Learn something useful in my chosen line

3. How many hours a day do you work and engage in activities that would help your career? ☐ 6hrs. ☐ 8hrs. ☐ 10 hrs. ☐ 12 hrs or more

4. How many hours do you spend to update yourself in your field, or acquire a skill in your profession?

   ☐ 1 hr. 2 hrs. ☐ 3 hrs ☐ 4 hrs.

5. Do you have a definite, time- bound practical goal in your life now?

   ☐ Yes ☐ No

6. Do you visualize from time to time having achieved your goals?

   ☐ Yes ☐ No

7. Are you always smartly dressed and groomed?

   ☐ Yes ☐ No

8. Do you move briskly all the time?

   ☐ Yes ☐ No

9. Do you sit, stand and hold your head straight and look up at someone you talk to?

   ☐ Yes ☐ No

10. Are you in the habit of making friends and keeping them?

    ☐ Yes ☐ No

11. Do you focus on your goals at least half the time you are awake?

    ☐ Yes ☐ No

12. Do you try to make your dear ones (partner/parents/children) happy?

    ☐ Yes ☐ No

13. Are you careful to drive away negative thoughts and drive in positive thoughts?

    ☐ Yes ☐ No

14. Do you try to focus on your strengths and positive qualities?

    ☐ Yes ☐ No

15. Do you believe you will succeed?

☐ Yes ☐ No

16. Do you keep your body fit with exercise and diet?

☐ Yes ☐ No

17. Do you think you are careful to exercise your brain and memory?

☐ Yes ☐ No

18. Are you careful in cultivating and maintaining good relationships with anyone you come across?

☐ Yes ☐ No

19. Do you try to do your present work much more than expected of you?

☐ Yes ☐ No

20. Do you have adequate income? Do you manage your finances well and save something for the future regularly?

☐ Yes ☐ No

21. Are you able to understand, evaluate monitor and control your emotions?

☐ Yes ☐ No

22. Do you try to understand the emotional set up of the people you come in contact with and give reposes knowing fully their emotional set-up?

☐ Yes ☐ No

23. Are you trying to do more than you are paid for in your job?

☐ Yes ☐ No

24. Do you take every failure as a feedback and go forward without taking it much into your heart?

☐ Yes ☐ No

25. Are you willing to take risks, especially, calculated risks?

☐ Yes ☐ No

Give marks as follows (Total Max. Marks: 58)

1. Yes: +5 marks; No: 0
2. 1-3: 0 mark; 4: +2
3. 1: 0 mark, 2: 1 mark, 3: 2 marks, 4: 5 marks
4. 1: 1 mark, 2: 2marks, 3: 3marks, 4: 5marks
5. Yes: 5 marks, No: 0 mark

6-25 Yes: 2 mark, No: 0 mark (except question nos 15 and 19 which carry 5 marks for Yes and 0 mark for No)

If you get 48 or more you will be most probably a huge success in life. If your score is less than 25 you have a long way to go.